The Test: De Gaulle and Algeria

By the Same Author

THE TEST: DE GAULLE AND ALGERIA

MY BROTHER DEATH

WHAT'S WRONG WITH U.S. FOREIGN POLICY

THE BIG THAW

SIT DOWN WITH JOHN L. LEWIS

THE TEST:
De Gaulle and Algeria

✝

C. L. Sulzberger

RUPERT HART-DAVIS

Soho Square London

1962

© *1962 by C. L. Sulzberger*

Almost all the material in this book was first published in the author's column, or in dispatches, in *The New York Times* and is reprinted by their special permission. Copyright © 1947, 1948, 1949, 1952, 1955, 1956, 1957, 1958, 1959, 1960, 1961, 1962 by The New York Times Company.

Printed in the United States of America

For Arthur, who admires the subject

Contents

	Chronology of Events	ix
I	Introduction: Man of Character	1
II	The Exile and the Republic	11
III	A Camel-shaped Cloud	39
IV	One-Man Democracy	73
V	The Age of Giants?	97
VI	The Great Mute Strives to Speak	129
VII	The Final Conspiracy	177
VIII	Down with Intelligence; Long Live Death!	195
	Index	223

Chronology of Events

1946

Jan. 20 — De Gaulle resigns as President of the Provisional Government of the French Republic

Oct. 27 to May 28, 1958 — Fourth Republic. De Gaulle in retirement at Colombey-les-Deux-Eglises, a self-sought exile from politics

1954

Nov. 1 — Rebel bands first attack in southeastern Algeria

1958

Feb. 8 — French bomb Sakiet Sidi Youssef in Tunisia as reprisal against Algerian rebel operations from that country

May 13 — Uprising in Algiers by civilians and army, protesting confirmation of Pflimlin as Premier. Generals Massu and Salan put in command

May 28 — Resignation of Pflimlin Government and death of Fourth Republic

June 1 — Investiture of de Gaulle as Prime Minister

Chronology of Events

June 3	Parliament votes to give de Gaulle full powers for six months and to enact constitutional reforms
Sept. 19	F.L.N. provisional government in exile formed
Sept. 28	Referendum approves Constitution of Fifth Republic by 80 per cent
Oct. 6	France's fifteenth constitution goes into effect

1959

Jan. 8	De Gaulle names Debré Prime Minister of Fifth Republic
Sept. 16	De Gaulle proclaims policy of self-determination for Algeria
Oct. 15	Stillborn plot aimed at putting in power a triumvirate of Generals: Zeller, Salan, Jouhaud

1960

Jan. 24-31	Week of the barricades in Algiers, when *ultras* sought to seize the city from French authorities
June 25-29	First negotiations between the French Government and the F.L.N., at Melun
Oct. 31	General Salan slips across the border into Spain
Dec. 10	Abortive plot seeking to arouse army sympathy and oust de Gaulle in favor of General Salan

Chronology of Events

1961

Jan. 8	Referendum approves de Gaulle's Algerian policy by more than 70 per cent
Apr. 9	O.A.S. forms as a result of secret talks among conspirators in Madrid
Apr. 22-24	Insurrection led by Generals Challe, Salan, Jouhaud, and Zeller
Apr. 23	Salan escapes from Spain to Algiers
Apr. 26	Uprising squashed. Challe and Zeller surrender. Salan and Jouhaud go underground
June 1	Challe sentenced to fifteen years in prison
July 18-29	Second negotiations between the French Government and the F.L.N., Lugrin
Sept. 10	O.A.S. tries unsuccessfully to assassinate de Gaulle

1962

Jan. 4	Salan calls for general mobilization of the O.A.S.
Mar. 8	Third negotiations begin between the French Government and the F.L.N., in Evian-les-Bains
Mar. 18	French Government and rebel Provisional Government sign cease-fire ending war after seven years and four months
Mar. 26	General Jouhaud captured in Oran and flown to prison in France

Not many of my French friends confess to being Gaullists. I live in Paris, and Gaullism hasn't been really chic since 1944, when this capital was liberated. De Gaulle is neither far enough left to suit the Paris intellectual, who claims to follow his mind, nor far enough right for the good bourgeois, who prefers to follow his heart.

The Left calls de Gaulle a Rightist. The Secret Army Organization says he is a Communist tool. He himself disdains categories, but I suppose one might, according to current history's yardstick, call de Gaulle a Centrist. While he is thus liable to complaints from both political extremes, he represents the mass will of his countrymen. He is sensitive to this popular force of French opinion and he also has a keen sense of history. The trend of history today favors the middle of the road, not only in France but throughout the West.

De Gaulle may not be chic for the intellectuals of Paris (and rare is the Parisian who doesn't claim intellectuality), but it may be asked: Where are the Paris intellectuals when the crises come? When chaos crept across the capital in May of 1958, the Parisians were with de Gaulle. When his Prime Minister, in April 1961, summoned all citizens into the streets to block, if necessary, an airborne invasion threatened from Algeria, they were again with de Gaulle. And they were with him when O.A.S. terrorists started to explode their plastic bombs.

But only on these crucial occasions have they rallied. In between, Parisians grumble that de Gaulle reigns but doesn't rule, that his only skill is in manufacturing crises so that he may then surmount them.

The account of de Gaulle's career that follows has its beginning in 1947 and continues for fifteen years, until the spring of 1962. It ends at a moment when de Gaulle and France are still engaged in a kind of guerrilla civil war against a secret army of dissident Algerian Frenchmen led by officer deserters. My story has been extracted from my own newspaper columns. It tells the tale of France, a country I love, through sad vicissitudes. And it tells the story of a man I deeply admire who seeks to lead his country out of its travail.

It has been my good fortune to come to know de Gaulle relatively well. In no sense can I claim to be intimate with him. Few people can, and not one of them is a foreigner. I first met him during the war; later, I began to see him infrequently in liberated France. Starting in 1947, I began taking notes of our conversations. Included in this volume are impressions and quotations, over the years, that have been entered on the record. Perhaps someday I shall be able to add more details that still must be considered confidential.

What interests me, in reviewing the material I compiled, is this compelling fact: The essential characteristics of the man and the fundamental concepts of his thinking have been amazingly constant. From the moment he fled his occupied country on June 17, 1940, an angular young brigadier general of little repute outside the military intelligentsia (already fascinated by the prescience of his strategic thinking), he was obsessed by determination to re-create a Great France. Hardly anyone thought this possible. Yet this visionary has succeeded to a considerable degree despite his unyielding way, or perhaps because of it. If he has been awkward with his friends, he has also been adamant toward his enemies.

Churchill, as everyone knows, complained once that of all the crosses he was forced to bear the heaviest was the Cross of Lorraine, the symbol de Gaulle chose for his cause. The General is astonishingly obstinate, as the United States has come to discover in its dealings with him. Moreover, he is most obstinate when his position seems weakest. His manner is also quite extraordinary. Since his extreme youth he has made a deliberate fetish of loneliness. A report on him during his term in military school remarked that already he was behaving "like a king in exile." With this noble, aloof air he combines a methodical single-mindedness and, occasionally, a display of slyness. Indeed, he is a master of the ruse. Many of his original supporters complain he tricked them, yet the fact is that he never made them any promises. The professional officer corps that gave him so much trouble claims he deceived it on Algeria. If he did so, however, it was by innuendo, not by pledges.

Certainly his bland, austere manner sometimes masks Machiavellian methods. He has ill-disguised contempt for politicians and for political parties. He has thrown them into disarray and cruelly forced them, time and time again, to sign away their fortunes on blank checks. He chose as his implement to smash the dream of a French Algeria one of its most ardent advocates, Michel Debré, his first Prime Minister. Then, when this paradoxical mission was accomplished, he dropped Debré.

Mixed with this subtle, *rusé* quality, there is a certain heavy-handedness in de Gaulle. His humor is heavy. During the war, in London, he and a few Free Frenchmen used to spend their evenings mimicking the leaders of Vichy France.

De Gaulle characteristically always played Pétain, the man who had been godfather to his son and who was later to be sent to prison by him. Once a friend who had known the General many years told me, to my surprise, that as a youth he was somewhat of a gallant. "What was his technique?" I asked. "That," he replied, "of the heavy cavalry."

De Gaulle re-entered Paris from wartime banishment on August 26, 1944, having insisted that French troops should penetrate the capital ahead of other Allied units. He formed an established government—although provisional—after elections in November 1945. And he resigned as President January 20, 1946, because the bickering coalition he headed refused to accept his ideas on a proper constitution and a sufficiently strong executive.

During the twelve years he spent in country solitude at Colombey-les-Deux-Eglises, he studied, reflected, wrote, and, in a way, matured. He seemed more pensive and more tolerant when he was summoned back to power in 1958 by a country, now tottering on the brink of chaos, that once more remembered this lonely exile. Dr. Adenauer later told me he thought de Gaulle had benefited from this long isolation; that it helped him to become what the German Chancellor called "the greatest statesman in the West." Perhaps. Surely he was, as a man, softer when he came back to Paris. Apart from anything else, he had, while writing his fascinating memoirs tediously with pen and ink, never dictating, achieved a brilliant literary style and perfected his odd but effective speaking manner.

Throughout my conversations with de Gaulle during the twelve-year interim I have discovered a remarkable consistency. He was always convinced the Fourth Republic would collapse, although sometimes his estimates were premature.

He was confident that when this happened he would return and assume control; accordingly, he never abandoned his private sense of mission which, in a way both romantic and mystical, he associated with the mission of France itself. For de Gaulle, France and himself have been not only inseparable but indistinguishable.

His policy was quite simply *la grandeur française*. The Great Nation of France was never, to his mind, to become merely part of a massive coalition; it was to be Great in itself and the leader of a renewed vibrant Europe. From the very first—even when he was the forgotten man at Colombey, disregarded by politicians, ignored by the press, scoffed at by cynics, and rarely visited by diplomats—even then, he intended to remodel French democracy, to shed its outmoded appendages, including those of empire, to discipline the army and subordinate its restlessness to civilian control. By the spring of 1962, he seemed on the verge of accomplishing these essential aims.

I do not mean to say that he has not abandoned some ideas and revised others. His old theory that labor-capital *associations* should replace normal employer-union relationships seems to have been discarded. He has been able to do little to satisfy his obsession that the economic role of the middleman must be reduced. Initially he seemed to waver on Algeria. Once he was back in power, he undoubtedly for a time sought to give contradictory impressions, to confuse his opponents and to prepare his forces for an inevitable test of strength. It was these contradictions that deceived many of his supporters. Some of them were drawn into opposition and others, less understandably, into open conspiracy. But always, it seems to me, he has represented the will of France and, ultimately, history's tide. That is important. In fact, as he would say, "primordial." He likes the word "primordial" and the reason why is evident.

The goal de Gaulle has set himself to win is not yet won. The O.A.S. in the spring of 1962 was still murdering and sabotaging both in Algeria and France. The plotters have already tried to kill him once—in September 1961. They may well try again. De Gaulle has such sublime confidence in his destiny that he is careless with his personal safety. It is rare that he ever thinks of death, although I have one letter from him mentioning the subject.

As a public figure de Gaulle gives the impression of being aloof, authoritarian, even sometimes not concerned with the problems of individuals. People complain: "Why doesn't he worry less about France and more about Frenchmen?" But as a commentary this is more neat than fair. He is, in fact, both a great gentleman, the greatest save for Churchill I have ever met, and also a gentle man. He is patient, thoughtful, and infinitely courteous in private relationships. At least, such has been my perhaps limited experience.

Let me recount an insignificant incident. Once when I went to see de Gaulle on a summer morning, I put on my dark glasses to avoid the sunny glare. My dark glasses are fitted with the same lenses as my regular spectacles, and often I forget I am wearing them when I go indoors. I forgot on that day and I entered the General's office wearing them. De Gaulle, who had had much trouble with his own vision and was later operated on for cataracts, inquired immediately if there was anything wrong with my eyes. Foolishly I said I had a very slight touch of conjunctivitis. Why in heaven's name I said this I still don't know. The General, at any rate, remarked he was glad it was nothing serious and then we turned to other, more important things. The next time I saw him was perhaps six months later. There was no bright sunshine, then, just a dull winter afternoon, and I had no dark glasses, only my regular spectacles. As soon as he had waved me to a seat, de Gaulle looked amiably at me and observed: "I am pleased to see your eyes are well again." I consider this exceptional courtesy, to say nothing of a feat of memory.

The reason I recall this unimportant episode is to stress the tender quality de Gaulle has chosen to obscure from public gaze. He is a thoughtful man who, even in periods of immense stress, always answers personal letters, often in his own handwriting. He showed a profound affection for his sick daughter.

De Gaulle is not yet truly known to the public, either of France or of the world. The best books on de Gaulle have been those by de Gaulle himself. Someday I am sure his friend André Malraux will write a superb biography, certainly a moving and flamboyant one. I asked the General once if he hoped to retire in a few years, after he had completed his schedule of reforms, and write a last volume of memoirs. "Retire, yes," he answered with a suspicion of weariness. "But not another volume." Like anyone, he finds writing tedious, though few can write as well.

Some time ago I investigated the statistics of the de Gaulle family and discovered that his six immediate forebears, his parents and grandparents, had died at the average age of almost eighty. This, of course, was during an era before scientific knowledge had added to the traditional life span of threescore years and ten. The general is now seventy-one. Together with a surviving sister, he is the last of five children. According to the Mendelian law, he should—accident or violence excepted—have several more active years. His admirers hope that in such time he can achieve his supreme goal—a stable, happy France, marked by both real and moral *grandeur*.

Some of my friends will grumble at these words and say: "*Hein!* It is *le grand Charles* who prevents just that. His is the long shadow that gets in the way." Let them say so. I prefer to look at the record, the record of his public acts and of his private thoughts.

Some thirty years ago, when de Gaulle was a junior officer, he was also a part-time author and journalist, writing military articles under a pseudonym for a Paris paper. At that time, in his first book, a revealing self-psychoanalysis, he wrote: "The man of character confers nobility on his acts."

Herewith, then, extending over one and a half decades, the record of a man of character.

TWO

The Exile and the Republic

February 1947

Monsieur de Gaulle is still very much of the political picture even though he is not currently in it. Since his unsuccessful campaign against the new Constitution he has been keeping out of the limelight.

But he has not decided just to retire and write his memoirs.

He would refuse to accept the Premiership and form another "political" Cabinet. He would specify that he required absolute authority for two years in order to achieve certain specific objectives, which he would outline in black and white in a rather concise program.

But he must have popular backing. Therefore his demands would have to be submitted to the people in a nationwide referendum. If he won, he would take over—obviously as a temporary dictator, no matter what other name would be originated. And, many Gaullists argue, there is nothing unconstitutional about this; the constitution does not say anything forbidding referenda.

Those who speculate along these lines argue that, although France is weak, she is nevertheless stronger in her inherent qualities than many foreigners think. This war, thanks largely to the Germans' diabolically deliberate scheme of selection, caused the loss of many of France's best men, not only in battle but by extermination.

However, France's power and morale, like all Europe's, although in a visible state of decline, is not necessarily in a permanent condition of decline. In the past there have been peaks and valleys of European history, and all one can be certain of at the moment is that this is a deep valley.

De Gaulle, they say, is the man who can find the path leading up to the slope. The future may test this chain of reasoning. France has had her Joan of Arc. She has also had her General Boulanger. The question now is whether she will have her de Gaulle.

June 1947

Amid the complex postwar stirrings and new games of power politics being developed in the uneasy world is a huge realm of primary importance which, as an entity, is rarely considered; that of resurgent Islam. Since the days of the Prophet Mohammed and his energetic followers, whose aggressive activities persisted through the Middle Ages, the Islamic world, as such, has been a negative factor in world affairs.

But today, during a period of nationalist resurgence supplementing that initiated after World War I, Islam is again on the march. The movement is not on a uniformly religious basis (there is no longer a caliph), but on a nationalistic basis in which the bond of religion plays a vital role.

Strong independence movements are now going on in Libya, Tunisia, Algeria, and Morocco, with the great powers keeping many fingers in the pie. From Cairo, where the Arab League has its headquarters, a diplomatic and propaganda apparatus continues to extend its activities, working for a free Palestine (under Arab control), a free Libya, Tunisia, Algeria, and Morocco.

Thus it is evident that as the Moslem world stirs and

seeks to implement slowly developed ideas of national independence, the great powers are going to eye the prospects carefully and seek to retain or increase their respective influences there.

Every move that is made in Indonesia or Palestine has its repercussions in Cairo or Rabat. Every political trend in London concerning Islam has its repercussions in Moscow, and vice versa. Geopolitically speaking, the Koran today lies between the Christian world of the West and the atheist world of Eurasian Moscow; whether it wills or not.

October 1947

During a long conversation with General de Gaulle in May 1947, in a small Paris hotel, I asked him how, tactically, he planned to come to power; whether he would accept the Prime Ministry if it were offered to him "early this winter" by President Vincent Auriol.

"I cannot forecast such things," he replied. "That is a question of tactics. If events force such a choice, the Constitution will have to be amended."

I said to de Gaulle that would take some time, perhaps at least a few weeks. He replied:

"Some events, such as those of 1940, show that a Constitution can be changed quickly, even in one afternoon. . . .

"To re-create Europe, the first condition is that France should be on her feet. France is a Western power and Europe is the symbol of Western civilization. Europe, to be restored, must be built upon occidental civilization. Such a Europe would be an element of strength and equilibrium. . . ."

I then asked de Gaulle if by this he meant that he endorsed the conception of a "United States of Europe." He answered:

"The name 'United States of Europe' is not a good one. It implies a federalized Europe. We cannot accomplish that in the same way as the United States has federalized its separate states.

"But it should be possible to build a Europe on the basis of treaties between the European nations and to establish a system under which they would systematically be meeting at conferences to study common economic, political and social problems. . . .

"It has always been impossible to organize such a Europe before. Always in the past one nation has sought to dominate the others.

"France, in the seventeenth and eighteenth centuries, attempted to do this. Then came England; then, during the last fifty years, Germany.

"But, for the first time, such conditions no longer exist. No European nation has the ambition or the capacity to dominate."

I asked de Gaulle what he thought of some persons' charges that the R.P.F. (Rally of the French People, his political organization) was merely an anti-Communist movement. He replied:

"Of course the Communists will fight us and of course we will fight them. They do not play a French game. But set this question aside. The R.P.F. is something more. It is an organization of Frenchmen to create and promote a French policy. . . .

"Naturally in a democratic system, such as I favor, there will always be political parties. But what is wrong at present is that the parties have all the powers, executive, legislative, and so forth. . . ."

November 1948

One of the biggest questions on the Continent of Europe is whether Charles de Gaulle will again come to power in France. If he does it will mean the end of the Fourth Republic.

Out of office nearly three years, the tall, serious-faced, religious General is today as much a man of mystery and as much a topic of discussion as when, in the early war years, he rallied the French people from London and North Africa and then, from 1944 to 1946, headed the Provisional Government of France. De Gaulle has recently stepped up his political activities. After refraining from extensive speaking tours for a considerable period this year, he has renewed his call for a general election, has made it plain he is ready to assume power, and has taken his cause to the people.

Upon the General's evident bid for control depends this country's course, perhaps for years to come. The future of Europe, the Marshall Plan, and the Brussels Pact are directly affected. And Europe's entire political development might well follow the trend of events in France.

What of the man who possesses such a tremendous power potential? What is de Gaulle like today? What does he stand for and who are his advisers?

The General, who will be fifty-eight on November 22, is an austere puritan, a devout Catholic, and a retiring family man. In this he reflects the background from which he comes —conservative, perhaps somewhat royalist, and very religious. He is scrupulously honest and no breath of personal scandal has ever been whispered about him—in contrast with so many other French politicians.

Sincere and studious, he has a psychological make-up which appears to prevent him from being close to many people. For the most part he does not call those who work intimately with him by their Christian names. He is a man who lives in reflective solitude for considerable periods of time. There are those who have visited his family circle in his country home at Colombey-les-Deux-Eglises who say that, sometimes for hours, the General sits wrapped in his own thoughts and silence reigns. He is certainly distant and haughty; that was the impression both Roosevelt and Churchill formed.

At Colombey he follows a simple, country gentleman's routine. According to some of his friends, he reads several newspapers each morning. Generally, he spends much time reading, even when he is actively engaged in public affairs.

As for his convictions, he seems utterly sure in his own mind of the rectitude of his thoughts, his analyses, and his conclusions. There is undoubtedly a streak of the mystic in him. He appears to have an unusual feeling of "oneness" with France and his own destiny.

Cool and distant as he may be in private conversations, he has a curiously magnetic personality. Persons who have visited him or attended small meetings where he was present have been struck by this, whether they agreed with his ideas or not. His mind is precise and, aided by a gift of particularly fine phraseology, he expresses his thoughts with special clarity.

But what actually is the political theory and application which de Gaulle wants to put into effect in place of the Fourth Republic?

De Gaulle himself told this writer last year:

"The aim of the R.P.F. is to group the French people in such a way as to permit a system in which policies can be decided and responsibilities assumed in the interests of France, independent of the aspirations of any single political party.

"The aim of the R.P.F. is the reconstruction of France to its full productive capacity and power. It is necessary to restore productive capacity, and in order to do so we must provide for full free enterprise. . . . It is necessary to increase the volume of French production. Simultaneously it is necessary to find a solution to problems relating the working of capital and labor."

How would de Gaulle come to power? And what are his chances?

First of all, he clearly counts on a final collapse of what he has denounced as the unstable party system as it has existed in the Third and Fourth Republics.

He counts on the advent of a situation where a fed-up public will demand stability as represented by himself and his movement. Whether he could secure power through an election or a plebiscite—if that moment on which he bases his hopes arrives—cannot be said. It is illogical to expect a parliament which contains many members who would not be re-elected to dissolve itself.

If legal means were not available, it is not impossible that the General might agree to unconstitutional methods to accomplish what he considers his mission of saving France. De Gaulle certainly has the authoritarian type of mind which is often associated with a military education and career. However, his term as head of the French state showed not the slightest sign that he sought to install an autocratic regime.

October 1949

General de Gaulle remains a factor in France's political picture and his ultimate importance cannot yet be accurately assayed.

It is worth summarizing his attitudes on various critical points. He himself feels that his views are nowadays insufficiently known, because, he contends, the present French Government deliberately seeks to exclude his opinions from the press and radio. He feels that the Quai d'Orsay's diplomatic representatives abroad deliberately seek to minimize his importance.

He believes that France is now convinced that the existing Constitution is inadequate and at the root of such political disputes as those of this month; that therefore the country would welcome a new constitution that he would offer to the voters as virtually his first act if and when he came to power.

The General declares, however, that he would prefer for France this difference: that the President would be able to choose his own Cabinet and to dissolve the national Parliament, but that his Government would be responsible to that Parliament.

General de Gaulle holds that, in principle, the North Atlantic security pact is a good thing for Europe and the world, but that the practical aid foreseen under the military-assistance program is quite insufficient. Furthermore, he feels that France is not doing enough to strengthen herself for this uneasy world.

The General feels that the future stability of Europe lies in a direct agreement between France and Western Germany on a basis of equality. He thinks that such an accord now between Bonn and Paris would offset the Soviet move in creating an East German state.

On the basis of these views, it is possible to predict the following definite trends should history bring him back to the position of chief of the French state:

A constitutional reform of drastic nature; an assertion of more independent and less conciliatory French views in international councils; a new policy toward Germany counter to the ideas entertained to date by Washington and London.

March 1952

General de Gaulle, now in his sixty-second year, has an extraordinarily complex character. Remote, arrogant, pious, and conservative by inclination, he has unusually few close friends, but a large circle of fanatical admirers. Although he has few of the usual popular attributes, he is keenly alert to the political temperature.

His personality is antipathetic to the thought of compromise. As a result, the General and his Rally of the French People, which claims it is not a party but behaves exactly like one, is playing its present game for the highest stakes—winner take all.

De Gaulle's fundamental policy is, "Security against the adversary, independence with regard to the Allies." By that he means that Europe must be protected against an initial Allied retreat in case of war; that France must command all forces on its national soil. He is prepared to negotiate directly with Bonn for the rearmament of Germany because he considers the proposed European defense force "a joke of the politicians."

The only role General de Gaulle apparently ever expects to play again is that of France's undisputed and accepted leader. He believes that the difficult world situation requires a "real national union around a man."

Thus, clearly his conception of personal authority is stronger than that embodied in the American type of Constitution which he so much admires.

June 1955

A full-fledged North African crisis is brewing. Guerrilla operations in Algeria are serious. Moroccan resistance to French administration and savage French colonialist reaction have increased. It is improbable that the return to Tunisia of the nationalist leader Habib Bourguiba, despite his accord with Paris, will completely subdue extremists.

What will be American policy if North Africa blows up? How will the United States reconcile the apparent dichotomy between its European and Near Eastern–African policies? The time is coming when it will have to adopt a decisive attitude. The Quai d'Orsay is not optimistic that it will favor France. And if that prediction is correct, it is indisputably certain that a serious crisis in Franco-American relationships will arise to plague the oldest transatlantic alliance and its successor, NATO.

August 1955

But France, overwhelmed by wartime conquest and therefore touchily compelled to seek prestige, has never faced the new realities. General de Gaulle's insistence that his country remain a great world power has been a psychological touchstone of the Fourth Republic.

But in neither Algeria nor Morocco is a solution in sight. There is a large French population in Algeria which is regarded juridically as part of metropolitan France, not a protectorate. Therefore Paris argues the solution is to "integrate" Algeria more closely into France.

It is a practical impossibility to absorb Islamic, African Algeria completely into Catholic, European France.

August 1956

The only gigantic figure on France's mid-century scene has been that of the sad and embittered de Gaulle. Now living out a self-imposed retirement on a modest village estate, the haughty General has, like the aged Churchill, turned largely to a literary career. Each day he works with painstaking precision upon his memoirs, writing in pinched, labored hand, undeterred by weakening eyesight, unwilling to dictate because he feels this hampers proper compositional balance. The result is elegant French prose.

De Gaulle's insistence on national eminence has not been recognized by the realities of an atomic age. In the Levant, in Indochina, in North Africa, the overseas empire cracked off and vanished into the anticolonial tide. And metropolitan France itself, despite a rising birth rate and a balanced internal economy, never managed completely to recapture the full vigor of political or productive energies.

Many attribute to de Gaulle himself considerable responsibility for these failures, which succeeded the romance of his Lorraine cross. Uncompromising, ill-adapted to harmonizing opposite views, he showed scant political talent.

While his eye was fixed upon the lofty dream of a great imperial France, his slowly recovering country lost opportunities in statesmanship.

In 1946 King Haakon of Norway observed to me that all the Continental lands were seeking French leadership to unite them as a bloc between the two extra-European superpowers; but that de Gaulle blindly ignored this chance. He insisted on playing a global role that France's energies were unable to fulfill.

The General toyed with odd political formulas like that of labor-capital *associations* reminiscent of the outmoded corporate state. He awarded high governmental positions to Communists before deciding, all too late, that they must be banned from politics as Soviet collaborators. He squabbled with Right and Left, disdained advisers, irritated allies, and infuriated many of his friends. Finally in 1946 he resigned his office, only to organize a strange nonparty coalition, the R.P.F., which failed.

For the better part of a decade, as France skidded from one political crisis to another, the gloomy General has sat stolidly upon the sidelines confiding sardonic observations to his callers, predicting pitfalls and disasters. Yet, removed as he is from the active stage, the very existence of his vigorous personality reminds many Frenchmen of a possible alternative if chaos ever comes. That alternative would be de Gaulle, vested with true executive authority.

Effective government is difficult in France because of its citizens' deep-seated suspicion of moves to develop the executive power. Experiences with dictatorship, headed by those of the two Napoleons, sometimes exaggerate French concepts of democracy to near anarchy.

A feeling of impotence has crept across the national consciousness, succeeding brave, brief dreams of postwar grandeur. Capital has fled or been secreted. Productivity is hit by lassitude. Unfair taxation has induced the resentments expressed by the pitiful Poujadist movement. Hurt feelings of nationalism inspire indifference with hints of xenophobia.

Only disaster in 1940 produced the solitary giant of this era in French history. And only when France was in its lowest depths was de Gaulle truly successful. Surely only another disaster could restore him to the active scene. Meanwhile France, led by sincere and able men but of no towering stature, engages in successive battles for survival as a factor in the world.

December 1956

The disastrous consequences of Anglo-French intervention in the Middle East in the unfortunate Suez expedition make almost inevitable a new development of considerable strategic importance—creation of another atomic military power. For France now realizes it must arm with nuclear weapons or relinquish any pretensions to major influence in world affairs.

The French General Staff has made precise calculations as to what is required and what the national economy can support. General Charles Ailleret, a forty-nine-year-old career officer who is *Commandant des Armes Spéciales,* estimates that within eight years France can produce a stockpile of seventy plutonium bombs. These would be manufactured on the following schedule: one in 1958, two in 1959, six in 1960, fifty in 1963, and seventy by the end of 1964. Ailleret believes an atomic submarine can be added to the French fleet by 1962.

The General reasons: Only the possession of nuclear arms enables a modern army to avoid presenting merely an expensive façade obliged to surrender to the least atomic blackmail. Furthermore, he argues that atomic weapons would permit France to assure its national defense on a far less costly basis than classical armaments.

Certainly it will be more difficult to fix international limitations when more nations are capable of nuclear military action. Even with small stockpiles, new atomic powers can touch off nuclear conflicts.

A French decision to turn its atomic-energy program into a military channel could have serious political consequences in Europe.

It is now clear, however, that the French General Staff sees for France a total lack of independence of action as long as it has no military atomic capabilities of its own. Therefore, one can virtually assume that strategic planning in Paris will henceforth be conceived on a more nationally independent basis. This would be less totally reliant upon the NATO alliance, which served only as a brake in Egypt.

June 1957

France maintains almost 400,000 men in Algeria—including combat troops that should be stationed in Europe under Paris's NATO pledges. But even with this power, plus helicopters and excellent road transport, it has been impossible to squash the insurrection. Hitting a partisan force is like punching a pillow.

Paris insists the military situation in Algeria has improved.

But it is not feasible for a civilized power, like France, to strike back with terror against terror such as that employed at Melouza. The world was aghast at the crime. But behind it lies a hideous, implacable revolutionary logic that bodes ill for both the French and the more moderate Algerian nationalists.

The use of terror has become orthodox strategy in guerrilla warfare, a brutal fact that lies behind the hideous Melouza massacre. One partisan group, the F.L.N., or National Liberation Front, slaughtered all the men of a village merely because they had first sympathized with a rival outfit, the M.N.A., or Algeria National Movement, and then had accepted French protection.

The purpose of this crime is obvious. It is intended to warn all Arab villagers against co-operating with French authorities. And it is meant as a demonstration of the F.L.N.'s ruthless determination not to tolerate rivals in the field of nationalism.

Blackmailing an entire population with savagery is, unfortunately, not new. During World War II, guerrilla organizations in Europe applied similar Draconian measures. In Yugoslavia, in Greece, and in Albania underground armies fighting Axis occupation also fought each other—over civilian corpses. For, it was discovered, sometimes it is possible to terrorize a population into sympathy if it cannot otherwise be won. And the aid of the passive, nonfighting masses is of crucial importance to guerrilla operations.

T. E. Lawrence, who guided the Arab revolt of World War I, wrote in the Encyclopaedia Britannica that insurrection can be applied against "a sophisticated alien enemy [in this case France] in the form of a disciplined army of occupation too small to fulfill the doctrine of acreage: too few to adjust numbers to space, in order to dominate the whole area effectively from fortified posts.

"It must have a friendly population, not actively friendly but sympathetic to the point of not betraying rebel movements to the enemy. Rebellions can be made by 2 per cent active in a striking force and 98 per cent passively sympathetic."

Yugoslavia's Tito and Greece's E.L.A.S. chiefs discovered that a people could be prodded by terror into the necessary condition of friendliness when, for one reason or another, it was not originally well disposed. In both countries the majority opposed the Axis forces. But their sympathies were divided between Communist and anti-Communist resistance bands. And each—in each country—often deliberately employed brutality to secure the required support.

Mao Tse-tung, who led a famous partisan campaign, summarized its military methods accordingly: "When the enemy advances, we retreat. When he escapes, we harass. When he retreats, we pursue. When he is tired, we attack. When he burns, we put out the fire. When he loots, we attack. When he pursues, we hide. When he retreats, we return. Our strategy is one against ten, while our tactic is ten against one."

These maxims are standard for guerrilla movements and have been so for centuries. It is necessary to have not only space into which a partisan force may retreat but also human space to obscure and sustain it. Such is provided by the inactive but sympathetic population.

What is now occurring in Algeria bears some military resemblance to what occurred in the Balkans during World War II. The F.L.N. is undoubtedly nationalist. But it has been penetrated by Communists to a degree as yet unknown. The Algerian Communist party disbanded itself and ordered its members to join the Liberation Front, even to renounce party membership as F.L.N. demanded.

The F.L.N., which perpetrated the Melouza massacre, is stronger than the rival M.N.A. Furthermore, it is more extremist in its demands vis-à-vis the French. In terms of what became familiar in Yugoslavia between 1941 and 1944, the F.L.N. somewhat resembles Tito's Partisans except that it isn't Communist led.

The M.N.A. is more similar to Mikhailovitch's Chetniks. Its military organization is weaker than the F.L.N.'s. And its political demands are relatively milder. It, too, is given to violence and has had success in organizing murders and strikes among Algerians living in France.

The French, caught between these warring nationalist factions, are having a miserable time. It is virtually impossible to liquidate a determined guerrilla movement when it has access to outside arms, as the Algerian rebels do from Tunisia and Morocco, and is supported at least passively by the masses.

France's Fourth Republic is about to experiment with its eighteenth government—following four provisional postwar administrations. The new Ministry comes in with little chance of success and much opportunity for disaster. For, politically, this is a sick country. Its manifold parties have perfected a disheartening form of executive paralysis. Their recondite game has attained a stage where it can be said of each successive Cabinet, first crippled, then ejected by the Deputies: When the water reaches the upper deck, follow the rats.

In the background sits the gloomy figure of Charles de Gaulle, preaching a kind of private pessimism rarely equaled since Jeremiah's day. The General foresees only disaster until he is brought back to power. And only disaster can possibly bring him back.

February 1958

France has been in a financial pickle for a long time, thanks to the Algerian drain. London is scarcely in a position to extend serious help. But Bonn is. As a matter of fact, in estimating where best to cast bread on foreign waters, the Federal Republic thinks first of France and then of India.

The French are very desirous of getting West German investment to help develop the Saharan hinterland in Algeria. While the Ruhr barons and bankers have played coy on such a project, they have by no means closed the door.

Furthermore, the French are determined to join the nuclear-weapons club, whose exclusive membership is now limited to the United States, the Soviet Union, and Great Britain. But manufacturing atomic arms is expensive business. Who can help out? Obviously Germany. The French have tested two missiles, Monica and Veronica. But their capacity to fabricate atomic warheads has yet to be proved.

The French and Germans already operate a joint rocket experimental station at St. Louis in Alsace. Nothing stands in the way of expanding such collaboration. It is no secret that France is pushing its nuclear program and could benefit from both German brains and money.

Undoubtedly many Frenchmen and many Germans fancy the idea of strengthening ties between their countries in order to counter what some describe as an Anglo-Saxon "condominium" in NATO. Nobody can at this time foresee how powerful this movement will become. But it does exist as a novel phenomenon in postwar Europe. And, as it gains in vigor, the old entente cordiale begins to weaken.

It is almost as cruel and bloody a process to relinquish as to make an empire. This old truism of history was learned successively by Rome, Madrid, Vienna, and Constantinople. Now again London and Paris are acquainting themselves with its sad, bitter verity.

Britain has advanced a long way toward transmogrifying imperial notions into some original and perhaps workable kind of cultural and economic association, the Commonwealth. But along the road there have been deep pools of blood: in partitioned India, in partitioned Palestine, in Malaya and in Cyprus. Disentanglement from the past is a difficult and often brutal process.

France, because its internal political system is so much less stable than Britain's, has suffered quite as much agony with far less success or promise of success in its attempts to move from old-fashioned imperialism to a new relationship with its colonies. Indochina proved a tragic military holocaust. The French managed to salvage little from the wreckage. And now Algeria, like some tragic cancer, eats into this country's heart and brain.

The French in North Africa show signs of losing what is left of their famous *sang-froid*. The Tunisian bombing incident simply doesn't make sense. In the name of warning and in the hope of destroying a few Algerian rebel installations, Paris's hot-blooded generals risk spreading a war that they have not yet been able to win inside its present more restricted area.

Americans should, of course, understand the emotional impulses that produced this savage, seemingly senseless act.

Old phrases such as "hot pursuit," to which we ourselves became accustomed during the Korean conflict, today punctuate the thoughts of France. This country has suffered heavy casualties and a distressing financial drain in the bottomless guerrilla pit. This inspires a mad sense of frustration. And madness is what the gods, according to legend, introduce as a precursor to destruction.

It is a traditional fault of generals that they fight wars with the sole objective of destroying an enemy, wherever they can find him, without thought of winning an eventual peace. One can only imagine that this type of cerebration produced the Sakiet Sidi Youssef raid.

For there can be only one enduring result of this idiotic act. That is to instill among Tunisians a far more bitter hatred for the French and a far more active sympathy for the Algerian rebels than anything they have hitherto expressed. If Bourguiba, a friend of the West, does not turn violently against Paris, he is bound to be replaced by someone who holds stronger sentiments.

Should this happen, it cannot be long before Morocco also changes its present temporizing attitude. For the sake of smashing a handful of rebels and an impertinent antiaircraft battery in Tunisia, some French military genius may well have diminished by geometric progression any chance his country has of securing the obviously necessary North African peace.

When Woodrow Wilson, a coolly reasonable man, unlocked the Pandora's box of nationalism forty years ago, he did not foresee that cool reason was the least element which would apply in solving the difficulties presented as, one after another, new groups of people demanded the right of nationhood and their old rulers fought to check the pace of imperial dissolution.

Behind the brouhaha and bluster of its somewhat lame explanations on the Tunisian bombing, the French Government is deeply embarrassed by this totally unnecessary tragedy.

The order, it appears, was given by a French colonel whose identity is being kept a guarded secret. The exact circumstances are not yet even known to most members of the Cabinet. But they are all fully aware that this horrible affair was staged at the precise instant of maximum embarrassment with minimum chances of gaining anything.

The question therefore posed is this: If one colonel can cause so much damage by one misguided decision involving only conventional weapons, what can other colonels commanding nuclear and missile detachments do to menace future world peace?

Perhaps the most insoluble problem posed by the Sakiet mess is that of individual judgment. Obviously no French Government wants to spread the Algerian war, to magnify the difficulties of an already difficult operation. Obviously, furthermore, no French Government wants to risk losing the diplomatic support of this country's NATO allies. Above all, no French Government would gamble on such negative results against the possibility of destroying one tiny Tunisian outpost when it was at minimal strength.

Already the army has, from time to time, shown hints of getting out of hand. During the past year four high-ranking generals have publicly differed with the Paris Government. One resigned, one was put on the shelf, two were given sentences of confinement.

What will happen to the anonymous colonel in Algeria who, if he did not actually contravene orders from higher up, certainly exceeded any authority he should have had? And, if he is not cut down to size, what will be the effect upon hundreds of other colonels in Algeria who are fed up with the way *la sale guerre* is going?

Two profoundly important repercussions have emerged from the Sakiet bombing. The Algerian civil war has now been "internationalized" willy-nilly, despite French efforts to the contrary. And it has been plainly demonstrated that Paris cannot simultaneously seek to hold the friendship of Tunisia and Morocco while pursuing a policy of repression in the area between.

In fact, if not in diplomatic fiction, the Algerian war was already being "internationalized." France had become embroiled with Egypt, Yugoslavia, and Poland over maritime arms seizures and searches. Its relationships with Morocco and Tunisia were directly affected. So were ties with the United States, some of whose weapons have been employed in the guerrilla struggle.

As a result of the latest crisis, it is no longer possible to shove the problem back under the rug of unreality which pretends this is merely a matter of provincial public order. Nobody can presume to tell France how to settle its deadly quarrel. This country is emotionally too charged. Since 1940 it has fought a series of unsuccessful wars in each of which French families sacrificed blood for *la patrie*.

But the Arab world is also emotionally charged. From the Persian Gulf to the Atlantic there are movements toward unity. Egypt and Syria have joined governments. So have Iraq and Jordan. And most of the Moslems inhabiting Tunisia, Algeria, and Morocco dream of amalgamating some day in a single federation of what they call the *Maghreb*.

It is unlikely that France or any other power will forever be able to thwart this movement. Nor is it sensible to try. The French, if they can only find their way out of the cruel Algerian labyrinth, should certainly be able to retain strong ties of friendship, culture, and economics with North Africa.

Despite chauvinistic talk about the United States ousting France from South Vietnam, the country's trade there is again paramount. Even in Pondicherry and the other tiny enclaves ceded to India, French culture remains primary.

The French have always spoken of their "presence" in North Africa. Perhaps this is because of their old proverb: "The absent one is always wrong." But England, in shedding an empire, finds solace in its own maxim: "Absence makes the heart grow fonder."

One accepted definition of the word "paradox" is: "An assertion or sentiment seemingly contradictory, or opposed to common sense, but that yet may be true in fact." In this sense contemporary France is an extraordinary land of paradox. Consider:

The Fourth French Republic was supposedly designed to avoid the weaknesses of its predecessor which collapsed in 1940. Yet it is modeled as closely as possible upon that Third Republic.

For a decade France has been in a state of colonial war. But it has never dared call for general mobilization. It needs more men and money to meet NATO obligations and simultaneously to fight in Algeria. Nevertheless it is preparing to reduce defense expenditures.

Many people, even Frenchmen, complain that France is

declining in vigor. But emigration is small; the quota is never filled. The birth rate is high and the population continually rises. An energetic, new, young generation has succeeded to political power. Last year French production increased at a greater rate than either Britain's or West Germany's.

A moderate so-called "third force" has run French policy for ten years with remarkable consistency. However, there is always a real possibility that France might suddenly grant power to neutralists who would pursue a line similar to Nehru's. And there is an almost equal threat of a potential Right-wing coup.

France is Western Europe's wealthiest land in terms of natural endowment. But almost every Government suffers nightmares of bankruptcy. Absence of foreign exchange would curtail imports, paralyze production, spread unemployment, stimulate social unrest, and produce internal upheaval.

The traditional *douceur de vivre* remains contingent upon handouts. Nevertheless, fanatically determined to prove itself a great power, France spends billions to make an atom bomb.

France's most agonizing foreign-policy question—Algeria—is not even classified as foreign. Its greatest North African friend, Bourguiba, is resented because he is too "French." The Tunisian President makes remarks that are acceptable only from someone bearing a French passport. The French claim to worship pure reason and abstract logic. They are the first, therefore, to recognize that the prevailing situation produces "a certain incoherence." But while being the first to recognize this fact, the French are the last to rectify it.

Few people apart from elected legislators doubt that Parliament has too much power. But to curtail this power, the Assembly must agree. This is one thing it agrees *not* to do.

Whenever the Deputies get fed up with a Government they unite sufficiently to oust it. And the Government lacks power to throw the Assembly out by asking for new elections.

This Administration would like to modify the electoral law and obtain a new kind of Parliament. Then it could at least reduce the number of Communists on the Left and reactionaries on the Right. But the Deputies refuse. The Premier cannot even pose questions for debate if Parliament won't accept them.

It is sad to observe that while the constitutional-reform debate has been taking place, hardly anyone has been paying much attention to it. The country is too engrossed in the latest North African crisis—in part precipitated by the political paralysis no one can end.

During the Crimean conflict with Russia, a French officer watched the gloriously foolish charge of Britain's Light Brigade. He remarked: "It is magnificent, but it is not war." Could not the same cold light of reason be turned on the functioning of democracy here?

When one observes the election of Communist Deputies by fewer than 40 per cent of a constituency's voters, or when one sees the resulting Parliamentary palsy, can one not say: "It is logical, but it does not work"?

THREE

✢

A Camel-shaped Cloud

February 1958

Were Hamlet to wander along the Seine these days he might regard the turbulent sky above the National Assembly and inquire of Polonius: "Do you see yonder cloud that's almost in shape of a camel?" And this is a cloud no longer the size of a man's hand, no little cloud. Arising from the sprawling deserts of North Africa, this cloud threatens to spread across all France.

For the problem it represents will not be settled by any pacification of angry Tunisians, by any establishment of an East Algerian No Man's Land or by the mounting of new military offensives against the ruthless guerrilla movement in that country. It will only be settled by basic decisions, decisions affecting French relationships with all former North African colonies. These decisions must be taken here in Paris.

What must these be? The experience of Britain in disengaging from extensive imperial appanages would seem to indicate that commonwealth, a real commonwealth of independent nations, is the only answer.

What is a commonwealth? In the current sense of that amorphous international community of which the Queen of England is symbolic head, this is difficult to define. The British seem to interpret it, with their pragmatic approach, as a group of countries vaguely associated by extensive trade, similar ideology and cultural heritage.

During World War II General de Gaulle, then representative of the Free French movement, seemed to foreshadow such development in France's empire. But the trend was curtailed. The French Union, as formed, was only a disguised version.

This disintegrated because France itself was not strong enough to frustrate postwar nationalism. Syria, Lebanon, Indochina, Morocco, and Tunisia gained independence. In North Africa only Algeria remains, tortured by insurrection, under the fictitious guise of metropolitan province.

Many thoughtful Frenchmen wish to heaven their Government could terminate the present costly war, encourage federation of Tunisia, Morocco, and Algeria, and embark on a new era of close association similar to Britain's ties with India. But this body of opinion has no cogent political expression.

France is governed by a regime which cannot, in the very nature of things, make bold decisions. The nature of things is the French Constitution. This allows Parliament to throw out any Government which dares to face the facts.

The result is virtual paralysis at the top and a free field for proconsuls. One after another these proconsuls, individuals or special agencies, get the nation into trouble. Their sudden acts—like seizure of a plane bearing Algerian guerrilla leaders or the bombing of Sakiet Sidi Youssef—are then reluctantly accepted by Paris.

This Government is only an acrobatic tour de force. It is incapable of practicing the surgery that French logic sees as necessary. Each crisis that arises is eventually met—too late.

France's armed forces have never represented true political power. There have been four successful *coups d'état* since the Revolution—by Napoleon I, Napoleon III, Pétain, and de Gaulle. In each case a military man, if Napoleon III can be so considered, led the movement.

The situation today is sinister although one would be hard put to find evidence of this in well-fed, seemingly contented France. The nation is industrious and filled with vigor. But it is mired.

Statistics prove that only a small minority of Algerians are actively combating. Yet such is the nature of guerrilla wars. While there are exceptions, as in France's own Vendée, Britain's Boer conflict, and the Bolshevik quashing of uprisings in Russia, most guerrilla wars are won by the minority.

There is danger here that governmental paralysis could produce the following. First, pro-French regimes in Tunisia and Morocco may be replaced by anti-French regimes, either through lead poisoning or despair. Second, the Algerian war might wind up in disaster.

There are hints of this grim forecast today. And one should never forget that as a symbol of this country's unquenchable pride there remains, stirring in the background, the noble, haughty, disdainful, and aspiring figure of de Gaulle.

March 1958

The political atmosphere in France is becoming tense and lugubrious. Upon the surface there are few signs of strain. Life seems generous and gay. And pleasant harbingers of spring are in the air. The countryside stirs with seasonal vitality; cities prepare splendid cultural displays, and even the Government manages to slide over successive crises.

But this year, unlike previous years, there is an ugly stirring underneath. It is as if one were to walk along the vine-clad slopes of Vesuvius and hear the mountain grunting deep inside. Does it portend imminent explosion? That is a question many Frenchmen ask.

A long series of unfortunate and unsuccessful wars—against Germany, against the Vietminh, against Nasser, against the Algerians—has frayed the national nervous fiber. The steady loss of territory has deeply hurt the national vanity.

As a consequence numerous unpleasant and unrepublican manifestations have appeared. Henri Alleg, a Communist French editor in Algiers, has just published a book called *La Question* which has revolted thousands of readers. This describes in nauseating detail tortures he suffered at the hands of paratroopers.

Three magazines were banned by censorship this week. In one of them, the liberal *L'Express,* the famous author Jean-Paul Sartre argues: "If we wish to put an end to these abominable and distressing cruelties, to save France and the people of Algeria from hell, there is but one way, always the same, the only one we have ever had, the only one we shall ever have: to open negotiations and make peace."

Many Frenchmen sense they are approaching a critical moment of history. The army is restive; Marshal Alphonse-Pierre Juin makes nationalistic statements. Other generals have actually risked flat disobedience.

De Gaulle himself has so far refrained from public statements. But he receives an increasing number of visitors. To them he indicates nothing but profound contempt for France's present Government, present policies, and present parties. He would surely wish to sweep them out were he ever to regain power.

How could he return? He has no organized political back-

March 1958

ing. His influence is only in the form of moral stature and past prestige. It would seem there are only two conceivable means of bringing him back. One would be if President René Coty asked him to form a government. This would imply suspending some provisions of the existing Constitution. The other would be by *coup d'état.* Thus both are illegal.

Would de Gaulle agree to a *coup d'état?* The answer is probably yes. He staged what he regards as coups in 1940, when he organized the Free French movement, and in 1944, in liberated Paris. There is no indication that he himself would sponsor such drastic action. But he would accept power from others. From whom? The army? Organized labor? Certainly not from the squabbling parties of Parliament.

The world picture might well change overnight by an electrical reappearance of this proud, aging French hero of uncompromising views and deeply religious faith in his country and himself. Yet just this possibility is once again beginning to be discussed in France. The effects of such a dramatic development upon the foreign policy of the United States would inevitably be profound.

Yesterday an enthralling drama opened in Paris. While Right-wing and Left-wing Deputies were snarling at each other and thumping National Assembly desks, thousands of policemen marched upon Parliament in a "demonstration," not a strike. Policemen are prohibited by law from striking.

This was the first sign of organized disorder Paris has seen since the armistice, if one excepts the occasional mass parades arranged by France's Communists. The policemen, who manifested in plain clothes, were demanding better bonuses for duty in areas of the capital endangered by terrorists among this city's large Algerian population.

The fact that they marched at all is significant, perhaps gravely significant. If anybody is aware he is breaking the law, it should be a policeman, especially 7,000 policemen.

Is this the first scene of a drawn-out spectacle? Or is it only a somewhat startling one-act play? In the answer to these questions lies France's future. For some two years General Charles de Gaulle has been telling friends that before he can return to power this country needs a "drama."

It has always been de Gaulle's contention that regimes never reform themselves; they disintegrate and collapse. Looking back over the types of modern French regime, he observes that the monarchy did not know the art of self-reform. Therefore it fell. The Revolution and Directoire suffered a similar fate. Bonaparte was wiped out at Waterloo because he could not adjust to national requirements. And so on through the Restoration, the Second Empire, and three republics. Is the Fourth Republic menaced?

As Gaullists read history's lesson, the "drama" of a regime's end is inevitably accompanied by chaos and at least some bloodshed. Furthermore it is foreshadowed by a deep and swift change in public opinion. Once de Gaulle studied the newspapers of 1815, when Napoleon returned from Elba and marched on Paris. The first headlines spoke of order being restored upon the Mediterranean coast. Then they admitted that "the tyrant" had reached Lyons. Finally they boasted, "His Majesty the Emperor is in Paris."

If public opinion must express readiness for drastic action before a coup would have a chance of success, de Gaulle's advisers reckon such expression could come in one of three forms. Either the army would gradually show it no longer intended to obey the Government. Or a general strike, provoked by noneconomic problems such as Algeria, must indicate mass discontent. Or widespread depression might cause mass suffering and provoke tumult.

None of these preconditions prevails. Yet it is conceivable that the police strike may indicate a fourth element of potential chaos favorable to a coup. This would be a breakdown in the processes of public order. If the Government cannot swiftly and efficiently make clear that it will not tolerate another uprising by its servants, it is obviously doomed.

The Gaillard Government is not corrupted by power. On the contrary, it is corrupted by the lack of it.

In French argot the phrase for prison van, or, as we call it, Black Maria, is *panier à salade,* a salad basket. It is years since Paris has seen so many salad baskets.

These hideous, cruelly shaped, and somber vehicles, protected by grills or wire netting, are used to transport both policemen and those whom they arrest. Suddenly they have become a commonplace in the capital.

All around the National Assembly there are salad baskets, drawn up in squat formations, filled with serried rows of gendarmes, riot squads, and helmeted Mobile Guards. Blankly the occupants puff bitter cigarettes or stare at colleagues patrolling outside on the wind-swept pavements.

At strategic points, near the principal ministries, in the vicinity of General de Gaulle's headquarters, close to the residences of more contentious politicians, are still more salad baskets and their darkly uniformed habitants. Some nights the lovely Bois de Boulogne resembles a military car park.

Parisians are notoriously unnervous people, as their

pedestrian customs testify. They are given more to sarcasm than resentment when traffic is stopped and taxi passengers summoned to show their documents. But nobody is quite sure what is going on.

Since last week's march against Parliament by 7,000 mufti-clad police, the Government has flown in emergency law-and-order detachments from as far away as Alsace and the casbahs of Algeria.

The atmosphere is disquieting. The present Cabinet teeters from precipice to precipice suspended between conflicting fears of a divided legislature.

The press inquires: Will this produce a crisis like the others that have marked the postwar era? Or will it produce *the* crisis? *The* crisis means a toppling of the present system of democracy.

The chaotic Assembly was given virtually dictatorial powers by France's present Constitution. But it has shown little ability to dictate other than confusion. Impotent and distressed, the salad-basket Parliament is a prisoner of its own disarray.

One English journal, the Francophile Manchester *Guardian,* comments: "Our fears for the liberties and well being of France are real. . . . Arbitrary powers have been extended from Algeria to France after insufficient debate. . . . Our fears must be strong if the gradual slide away from truth and freedom continues."

France has a profound tradition of liberty and individual rights. But when viewed in terms of political fragmentation, one might say this has been almost excessively applied.

The United States desperately wants to help its oldest ally, which is today the heart of NATO's Continental complex. But, at the same time, it feels it cannot continue indefinitely to watch the threatened drift of all North Africa away from the Western fold.

Therefore, both in Washington and again at the Manila SEATO talks, Secretary of State Dulles told the French that 1958 is the last year in which to arrange an Algerian settlement. If such is not reached, United States policy may be faced with the need for what the Secretary calls "agonizing reappraisal."

Any decision in Algeria can never be arrived at without a strong hand in Paris. This does not exist. Infirmity is only perpetuated from brink to brink by indecision in the bickering Chamber of Deputies.

Local by-elections have shown a distressing drift by public opinion to the extremes of Right and Left.

These are curious, unexcited, but worrisome days in Paris. Hideous old slogans have been exhumed from a past the nation has endeavored to forget: "Death to the Jews"; "Into the Seine with the Deputies." The Cabinet strives desperately to gain enough authority to stabilize the situation. Unfortunately, government by salad basket is no answer.

April 1958

The only novel aspect of France's present political crisis is that a new generation of Frenchmen can now be seen to have inherited the insoluble problems of its parents. Félix Gaillard, whose resignation was forced last week, is the first Premier born since World War I.

He represents that brilliant, bored galaxy which has suddenly emerged in the arts through Françoise Sagan and Bernard Buffet, in fashions through Yves St. Laurent, and in politics through Maurice Faure, Jacques Chaban-Delmas,

Maurice Bourgès-Maunoury, and Gaillard himself. This is the youngest generation ever to assert itself in French history.

But the sad thing is that France's intellectual talents, handed down so successfully from father to son, have not resolved basic governing difficulties, likewise handed down from father to son. The same weaknesses that crippled the Third Republic now cripple its successor.

The reasons are not difficult to discern. Almost every competent observer arrives at the same diagnosis. Herbert Luethy, a shrewd Swiss analyst, writes in *France Against Herself*: "The great revolution and all the little ones which followed it have left in their wake the myth of the uncompleted revolution, which comes continually in conflict with the legitimacy of any existing order."

Alexander Werth, an Englishman, says in *France 1940–1955:* "Counter-revolution is a permanent reality in France, and its outwardly complete, though temporary, triumph at Vichy is much more than a historical curio."

And the American David Schoenbrun, in *As France Goes,* speaks of the traditional political fragmentation that divides this country. He refers to the "classic dream of a French politician to head a party composed only of himself and just enough voters to put him in office."

This fragmentation, while reflected in a shifting party kaleidoscope, retains a curiously consistent aspect of three main groupings: Right, Center, and Left. It is the struggle between those who wish to turn the political clock back, those who wish to move it forward, and those who would keep it approximately where it is that is the fundamental struggle this generation has inherited.

The extreme Left today is expressed by the Communists.

They have maintained a strong party organization. Some five million Frenchmen steadily vote to back their candidates. The Communists look to Moscow for inspiration.

The Right, mirrored by an oddly conflicting mixture of parties, tends to look through its Catholicism to Rome. And the Center, which, paradoxically, embraces both clerical and anticlerical factions, finds sympathy in Washington.

Each of these coalitions has had its moment of rule. The Left came in through the Popular Front before the war. The Right had its purest expression during the unhappy days of Vichy. And the Center has remained in unsteady power since the Fourth Republic came into being.

But there has never been a clear-cut and definitive victory by any one of these groups. All of the battles left unsolved by revolution seventeen decades ago still continue: between Right and Left, between progressives and reactionaries, between clericals and anticlericals.

As France has slipped down the power scale, internal quarrels debilitate it. No dynamic new leadership has been able to institute a fair tax system, rearrange agricultural and industrial inefficiencies, modify an economy of high prices and low wages, or create the necessary mass housing program. Recently revived finances falter. Strike threats are developing. The Algerian war continues to bleed the nation. And extremists talk of national "honor"—an acetylene torch which can be applied to anything.

May 1958

It has long been evident that the lowering Algerian storm would someday sweep northward. And it was equally evident that when it was blown across France's sweet fields by the high winds of destiny, its political epicenter would focus on de Gaulle.

This has happened. The chances are increasing that the proud, disdainful General may soon again become master of his country's fate.

More than two months ago I wrote: "The last time de Gaulle threatened to come out of retirement and seize the helm in France, one of his supporters complained: 'He marched us to the Rubicon; and then he told us to take out our fishing rods.' If there is another movement to the Rubicon, it will be no angling party."

This is no angling party. On the surface, delightful Paris appears as gay and insouciant as ever. But rumbles of danger echo underneath.

The unhappy regime, fighting with all traditional democratic means, struggles to assert its power. A state of emergency has been declared, although rubbernecking tourists do not know this. Meetings are banned. Unimportant police stations in the capital are closed so their forces can be mobilized at key points.

Nevertheless, France lies all too helpless before those who would employ unconstitutional methods. This is increasingly a struggle between the extreme Left, which clamors for a Popular Front, and the Gaullists, over the Fourth Republic's sickening body.

Trade unions have ordered labor to prepare to protect democratic liberties. The Socialist party announces: "The Republic is menaced." And in three successive directives the Communist Politburo has commanded workers to rally in factories, towns, and villages and not to allow "fractionalists" to gain control of the streets.

The Government has, in theory, cracked down on the

May 1958

Right. It decreed dissolution of a handful of ragtag and bobtail hoodlums' groups that specialize in chalking up provocative slogans and baiting the gendarmes.

But the real Right, to which the Center is rapidly gravitating, looks increasingly toward de Gaulle. And de Gaulle sits quietly under a "protective" security watch in his distant country estate. He awaits the moment of "drama" which he has so patiently, for so long a time, insisted would eventually encompass his return.

There is not the slightest proof connecting him with the sudden coup that flared up in Algiers. For the record, this would seem to have been an unplanned military *Putsch* led by a bunch of disheartened desperadoes.

Its leaders are impressive bullyboys. General Jacques Massu rejoices in the nickname "Roughneck" and a beak which his admirers liken to that of Cyrano de Bergerac. One of his colleagues, Colonel Jean Thomazo, is known as "Leather Nose." Another, paratrooper General Jean Gilles, heads an outfit known as the "Agile Rabbits."

Did these men alone decide to seize the helm? That is hardly likely. Massu has the political brain of a pumpkin. But behind him and beside him are shadowy agents of civilian leaders who owe allegiance to de Gaulle.

This is undoubtedly a deep conspiracy. Mysterious arrests are taking place. De Gaulle's old hatchet man, Jacques Soustelle, is under surveillance. General Lionel Chassin, one of the air force commanders, has simply disappeared. And the head of all armed forces, General Paul Ely, resigned—then reappeared in office. Nobody quite knows tonight through whom to channel military orders.

Thanks to efficient police dispositions, Paris has been rendered safe although many political cliques have arms.

But what about France? The bulk of the army and all its striking force are in Algeria. So is the air transport command. If anybody dares send the popular paratroopers northward, would they be seriously resisted?

A distinguished general, known as an opponent of de Gaulle, assures me: "The only reality is the choice between de Gaulle and a Popular Front. This is the only reality, whether you like him or not. The police and the army won't fight for a Government that doesn't exist."

De Gaulle himself, in splendid isolation, attends the climax he has so long foreseen. But he has made no secret of his willingness to accept power by any means. One means he contemplated was "failure of the army to obey the regime."

France's President, René Coty, a quiet student of history, is impressed by the fact that since the days of Caesar the inhabitants of this lovely land have demonstrated a certain instability. Caesar himself referred to the unstable Gauls.

For this reason the Republic's titular head prefers to see the French governed by a flexible system able to absorb sudden shocks and shifts in popular opinion. But what he wants is flexibility, not weakness.

In contradistinction to General de Gaulle, who has always called for a dominant presidential executive, Coty tried quietly behind the scenes to encourage constitutional reform giving to the Prime Minister, not the President, more authority over Parliament but keeping the Premier the servant of the legislature.

The President shares the average Frenchman's suspicion of too strong a central power. For the Frenchman, the state, in a sense, is the enemy. These sentiments evidently make Coty reluctant to even consider calling upon de Gaulle to save the situation. By historical instinct he mistrusts the authoritarian aspirations and philosophy of government attributed to the General.

The position of postwar France, liberated from tyranny and occupation, has curiously followed the pattern of another France, the First Republic of the Revolution. That endured until Napoleon's *coup d'état* of the Eighteenth Brumaire.

A historian, James Matthew Thompson, describes the era preceding the Bonapartist *Putsch* as follows: "The period was one of exhaustion, during which France gradually absorbed the shocks and countershocks of Girondism and Jacobinism, royalism and republicanism, democracy and bureaucracy, liberty and compulsion, till it was too weak to oppose the regime of the Consulate. The coup d'état of Eighteenth brumaire claimed at once to abolish and to consummate the Revolution."

The *coup d'état* that has now occurred in Algeria likewise pretends both to consummate and, in effect, to abolish the Republic. And like the maneuver that produced Napoleonic rule, this plot was evidently organized from within the Government as well as from without. Like Bonaparte, de Gaulle had evident supporters among those in power, above all in the army.

Despite glorious dreams of reinvigoration and global influence, despite an industrious and intelligent population, despite natural wealth, and despite huge injections of American economic aid, the France of recent years remained weak and divided by forces similar to those that eroded the country before Napoleon.

In a recent series of articles entitled "Simple Thoughts for Has-Beens," Hubert Beuve-Méry, Paris's most brilliant editor, called France's failure to solve her postwar problems "a monstrous and incomprehensible scandal. If there is not too brutal a shock," he wrote, "a regime condemned to death can stumble on."

But the brutal shock has come. And, as with that shock which all too recently destroyed another republic in Spain, it came from Africa. The force that brought Franco to Madrid was generated in Morocco. The force that seeks to push de Gaulle back into destiny's forefront was generated in Algeria.

Those who have been working to upset the established regime—and they are many—were right to center their efforts in Algeria. This is the scene of France's greatest drama. And the main French military striking force, a potential source of real power, is centered there.

Already before the coup began, Jean-Paul Sartre, speaking of democracy's degradation, warned: "The real Government is in Algeria." Georges Bidault, a Rightist former Premier, told his countrymen: "Let the Republic perish rather than French Algeria."

It was an officer in Algeria who, employing a Napoleonic phrase, *"moi, Général Massu,"* touched off the explosion. It was another general, Raoul Salan, commander of all Algerian forces, who announced after the coup began: "Algeria will save France."

Coups d'état are rarely improvised upon the spur of the moment. There must be wide complicity. And yet, when this plot first began to show its hydra heads, the authorities were astonished. They discovered that many critical branches of administration were riddled with conspirators.

The symbol of the present intrigue, General de Gaulle, is no Napoleon. He once controlled all sources of French power and made no effort to employ them. But neither is he a republican, in the sense that is familiar to the French.

The Government prefers to believe, or to pretend to believe, that the military coup in Algeria is not a coup against itself. Yet every leader of that action has been making totally seditious statements. The heads of the insurrection that is officially not an insurrection seek to bypass Parliament along clearly unconstitutional lines.

The legend is preserved that the army is not truly involved in politics, is united, and remains loyal to the regime. But General Ely, who recently resigned as Chief of Staff, issued a still unpublished order of the day in which he did not even mention the Republic. Two of his principal generals have been rusticated. They are neither free nor under real arrest. Another, General André Petit, ordered himself to Algeria and didn't come back.

There is similar unreality about the evident political leader of what is so obviously an extensive plot. Soustelle was under house surveillance in Paris. A story has been put about describing his dashing Fancy Dan "escape" in the best Dumas tradition. Nobody bothers to remember that the Paris police prefect's main adviser is a Soustelle adherent. Both he and the prefect stay in office. And, although Soustelle clamors to oust the Government, he has been charged with no crime.

Algeria itself is mesmerized by the odd shadow performance. The civil war has momentarily assumed a secondary role. Moslem crowds pour from the fanatically nationalist Casbah quarter of Algiers to demonstrate beside French nationalists. And the Paris Government, which ordered a ban on travel to the secessionist area, amiably arranged for a planeload of correspondents to fly there straight from Paris.

No official from the Premier on down has dared brand the patently rebellious leaders as rebels. And the Communists, who have been issuing manifestoes ordering protests in the streets and factories, managed only the palest imitation of a strike.

General Salan in theory acts for the Government as commander in Algeria. He solemnly insists the coup "is not a coup or an action against the Republic." Nevertheless he associates his person with demands for a de Gaulle Administration.

De Gaulle himself, whose shadow dominates this weird charade, emerges from self-imposed isolation only to utter cryptic statements that might have been the envy of Delphi's enigmatic oracle. He blesses the Algerian conspirators who wish to upset the will of Parliament. He implies that should he come to power he would scrap the present party system. Yet he speaks, as it were, in the name of the Fourth Republic.

De Gaulle sets himself up as a neutral arbiter. Is he truly neutral? Is it coincidence that Lucien Neuwirth, spokesman of the Algerian Committee of Public Safety, visited the General just before leaving for Algiers? Is it accident that those who claim to act on de Gaulle's behalf, without his knowledge, should demand that he "arbitrate" the day before he offers to do precisely that?

Surely these are astonishing coincidences. And, in a fascinated daze, the people of Paris virtually disregard the incredible clusters of *gendarmerie* and queue for theater tickets and potatoes.

Dynamic forces are poised unsteadily upon a brink of

violence. Can they continue so tenuously balanced? Is it possible for shadow and pretense indefinitely to obscure substance and reality? De Gaulle warned that events may *lead* to grave crisis. Is not the crisis already here? Is the way a republic can end not with a bang but a whimper?

The greatest paradox in this paradoxical French crisis is the position of the army. The army is the only remaining cohesive force in both metropolitan France and Algeria. It argues it is not involved in conspiracy against the Republic. But it endorses de Gaulle's implied conception of that Republic: *"La République, c'est moi."*

The French army prides itself on a tradition of avoiding politics. It teaches its officers allegiance to the Republic. Yet even Marshal Juin, France's senior officer, announces he has "no more confidence" in the regime.

This country's political Right has never been able to impose its will on Parliament since the crisis of 1934. But the army command, presumably speaking for that Right, seems to be attempting such an imposition of will by mounting blackmail pressure.

The Pretorian Guard is the elite of parachutists. This provided the backbone for the Algerian *Putsch*. The Government worries almost every night when rumors start about a sudden airborne descent on Paris. The only forces maintaining security around the capital are the police deployed beneath the chestnut trees. But just two months ago some 7,000 of these same police, wearing mufti, marched on the Assembly hollering "Into the Seine with the Deputies."

Operating as a power within the state that in effect seeks to reform the state, the army insists it is not plotting. But, in the same breath, it specifies its own conditions for settling the impasse. Today the only solution it considers acceptable is de Gaulle's return.

This was not true a fortnight ago. Even nine days ago, General Ely thought a strong Government without de Gaulle was possible. Three days later he had changed his mind.

Neither by sentiment nor by recent tradition has the army been Gaullist. But it has suddenly swung its influence behind the General. It now considers his person, his prestige, and his concepts the only logical answer to the problems of France and Algeria.

The Pflimlin Government and its predecessors handled the army with amazing obtuseness. Successive ministries were aware of a deep swell of military discontent. High officers complained: "For eight years, in Indochina, in Algeria and in Suez, we have been killing and been killed. We have been betrayed by weak Cabinets in Paris. Victory has never been attainable. It makes us sick."

Two months ago Ely cautioned Premier Gaillard that the army in Algeria might soon begin to ignore Paris. More recently he warned that administration in North Africa was on the verge of breakdown. Anybody familiar with de Gaulle's views knew he calculated that such a situation might be one means of projecting him to power.

Tuesday night, May 13, Ely went to Pflimlin and, in his presence, telephoned General Salan, commander in Algeria. He issued two instructions: to avoid bloodshed; and to restore order.

De Gaulle sent word to Ely that he wished to see him. Ely told this to Pierre de Chevigné, Chaban-Delmas's successor as Minister of Defense. He advised Chevigné that he intended to visit de Gaulle at his country retreat on Thursday

—in full uniform. "I cannot go clandestinely," he said.

Chevigné begged Ely not to see de Gaulle until after Friday's Assembly meeting, when the Government was to seek additional powers. So Ely postponed his trip until Sunday. But he resigned Friday. Consequently he sent an aide to tell de Gaulle he would not come. He was no longer Chief of Staff; a talk would be meaningless.

Ely's resignation was precipitated by a folly. Without advising the Chief of Staff, Chevigné arrested Ely's two principal assistants. One, General André Martin, is again at liberty and serving. The whereabouts of the other, General Maurice Challe, are unknown.

In a fury, the dignified Ely resigned. He felt he could no longer serve this Government loyally. Furthermore, he did not wish to give the impression that, by continuing as Chief of Staff, he disapproved of the Algerian uprising or the role played by Salan and Massu.

Above all, Ely wished the army to remain consolidated on both sides of the Mediterranean. He issued a final order of the day demanding that all troops maintain "the cohesion and unity of the French Armed Forces, the supreme pledge of national unity."

Invisibly the army is closing ranks. Officially it pretends to stand aside from politics. This intention has become a fiction. The army wants de Gaulle—and quickly.

Everything seems over with the Fourth French Republic in the precise form familiar to us. That is to say, everything seems over but the shouting—or the shooting. This aspect will soon be clarified.

From the start of his brief authority, Pierre Pflimlin was faced with issues too big for him. May 13, while Gaillard was winding up as head of a caretaker Cabinet, General Massu telephoned from Algiers for instructions. He told the outgoing Premier a mob had formed and intended trouble. Should he shoot, he inquired. No, said Gaillard.

Next morning the Prefect of Oran called the Premier's office with an identical problem. This time the answering voice was Pflimlin's. He had just taken over. "Do not shoot," said Pflimlin.

That was the brief moment of decision. Therefore, presumably, it had been selected by the plotters for their first dramatic test. Horses were changing in midstream when the conspiracy struck.

Ever since, during a confused fortnight, whatever initiative Paris might initially have gained by ruthlessness was dissipated by inaction. For the sake of avoiding bloodshed the regime chose to appear as if it supported the intrigue against itself.

Pflimlin was in the position of a man who finds a burglar rifling his safe. At gun's point, he tells the intruder to continue. Later he announces: "I wasn't burgled. The man was acting on my instructions."

The process of disintegration has been steady. A surface show of force was mustered in the Republic's name when the capital filled with massive police concentrations. Even then officials conceded privately that Paris could not be held against any descent of paratroopers from Algeria.

Jules Moch, the tough old Socialist who once broke Communist riots, was Minister of Interior. But his famous will power seemed paralyzed. No organization was rallied to fight for the Republic. Only the Communists, somewhat frightened and halfhearted, talked tough.

Helmeted *gendarmerie* are still under the chestnut trees. But they are unlikely to battle for this Government against anyone but Communists, certainly not against de Gaulle.

For days the Assembly has been passing ritual resolutions. For all their significance these might have been endorsing motherhood. One of Parliament's rare unanimous votes expressed gratitude to the army—already engaged in obvious insurrection.

Some politicians began acrobatic swerves in an effort to catch the accelerating Gaullist band wagon. Others took slight pains to disguise conspiratorial aims.

The day before he fled to Algiers, Pascal Arrighi, a Corsican Deputy, told friends he was off to Taiwan. He showed his passport with a Chinese visa. That same passport included a wad of American dollars. "Why do you need so much money on a free official journey?" he was asked. Arrighi had the grace to blush. Today he is in seclusion in insurrectional Corsica.

Many worried Frenchmen hope the hand-over to de Gaulle will be efficient and, above all, quick.

The Government's understandable reluctance to let in de Gaulle with even the appearance of legality will increase the influence of Rightist forces revolting in his name, and the stronger these forces become, the more difficult it will be for de Gaulle to quell them—once this becomes his responsibility.

A miasma of incipient terror has lifted from Paris. The capital is still glutted with leaden police concentrations. Secondary airports are blocked by barbed wire. There is a surly undertone of grumbling in the Red belt. And the unhappy Parliament, so fittingly decorated with that style of mural painting known as *trompe l'oeil* or "illusory," echoes failure.

But the nightmare of violence has been swept away by a Gaullist wind. The splendid Place de la Concorde, where hard-bitten Frenchwomen knitted beside the guillotine during this country's great revolution, presented a different aspect last night. No grim harridans clacked needles to the slicing off of heads. Instead, automobiles massed up, tooting frenetic horns in honor of de Gaulle. The noise violated a strict city ordinance. And the sentiment violated the Fourth Republic.

In effect, what this noisy sentiment meant to indicate was sudden endorsement of the *coup d'état* in favor of the General. Everybody has chosen, with remarkable self-deception, to avoid use of the embarrassing phrase. Yet it was a coup that ended the regime.

On the whole, de Gaulle foresaw these extraordinary happenings with clarity. He always insisted he would not return unless he held "real power." To obtain this, he prophesied, events must become sufficiently dramatic to disintegrate the system. He never thought it would reform itself. None of thirteen different French regimes during a century and a half reformed itself in time.

De Gaulle recognized that, politically, President Coty did not have power to call him to authority—but that, in actuality, he could if he so wished. To bring about such a situation, drama—one of the General's favorite words—was first needed.

Drama, to him, did not require war. Some form of tumult might suffice. For example, in 1830, Charles X and the Restoration disappeared without war. So did the 1848 Republic.

Nevertheless a variety of chaos was necessary. De Gaulle considered that this regime had been made despite him and "against" him. He therefore stubbornly refused to lift a finger to preserve it.

A fiction has grown up that de Gaulle himself would never be party to any *coup d'état*. The General is more honest than his admirers.

Of requisite preconditions for a coup, de Gaulle always reckoned on two as the more likely. Either the army would decide no longer to obey the Republic, or there would be a general strike provoked by exterior events, such as the Algerian crisis. The first occurred. It was no spontaneous accident.

By the time France's air force bombed the Tunisian village of Sakiet Sidi Youssef last February, the General realized military anarchy was approaching. He noted that special intelligence services, on three successive occasions, had taken highhanded measures. First came the seizure of an airplane carrying Algerian rebel leaders. Second came the grab of a Yugoslav ship containing arms. Third came Sakiet. In each instance, de Gaulle noted, the Government weakly accepted independent actions by its proconsuls.

He concluded there was no longer any Government, only people who inhabited the palaces of the Government. The army was restive. But would it rise?

Without the army, it is perfectly apparent, de Gaulle could not have come to power now. As he foresaw, in the end he also had the people—or considerable numbers of them. That was meant to be the significance of last night's carefully promoted klaxon chorus. Will the people still support de Gaulle when the army presents its bill for services rendered?

June 1958

The United States has made a powerful effort during the past few days to indicate how much it admires General de Gaulle. President Eisenhower said he likes this haughty Frenchman. Secretary Dulles intimated pleasure that France would assert more "independence" in world affairs.

Eisenhower's statement is not contradicted by his wartime memoirs, although, in addition to confiding that "I personally liked General de Gaulle," he saw in him "hypersensitiveness and an extraordinary stubbornness in matters which appeared inconsequential to us."

Dulles's statement, which seems amiably tactful, unfortunately managed to irk some important Frenchmen. Being touchy these days, they inquire: "Does the Secretary think we haven't been 'independent' in the past? Does he think we've been working for America, not France?" Allowance must be made for raw nerves.

The fact remains that Washington, like most capitals, was late in realizing that de Gaulle was again beginning to dominate the French scene. Only two ambassadors from NATO countries—and two from the Communist bloc—were truly on top of this dramatic development.

The United States has been wrong on the most significant occurrences in postwar France. The first was the fate of the European Defense Community. The second was de Gaulle's political resurrection. The State Department obstinately assumed E.D.C. would be ratified by the French Assembly, even when powerful evidence pointed to the contrary.

Likewise, until very recently, U.S. diplomats were selling de Gaulle short. They just didn't think he had any chance of coming back—until the beginning of May. The only branch of the Government to analyze the General's chances accurately was the Central Intelligence Agency.

There are reasons for U.S. diplomatic myopia. The first was wishful thinking—and this is somewhat bitterly recalled by de Gaulle himself. It was thanks partly to skillful American political intervention that he was prevented from reassuming power a decade ago. The U.S. strongly supported a "third force" coalition to keep him out of office.

Another explanation is the structure of French society. Diplomats tended to garner information in Paris largely from Cabinet Ministers, from parliamentary Deputies, and from those who habitually hang around fashionable embassies. But none of these groups, for many months, have known what was going on.

The United States has not been alone in such miscalculations. Its embassy, since October, was aware that something was rotten even if it didn't imagine de Gaulle as the answer. And Sir Gladwyn Jebb, the polished British Ambassador, visited the General in March and came away unimpressed.

Four diplomatists were more precise in their previsions. These were the Turkish Ambassador, Numan Menemençioglu; the Italian, Pietro Quaroni; the Russian, Sergei Vinogradov, and the Pole, Stanislaw Gajewski.

Menemençioglu, a wily veteran, who had been his country's Foreign Minister, retired two years ago and died last February. But while he was active in Paris, masquerading as a lazy card player, he kept a sharp eye on the political forest, ignoring the trees. Above that forest he always saw the looming figure of de Gaulle.

Quaroni likewise perceived the future shrewdly. Before

he was transferred to Bonn on April 1, he forecast de Gaulle's return. Most of his colleagues heard his observations with skepticism.

Vinogradov and Gajewski were in a somewhat different situation. Possibly they had private intimations from the massive Communist intelligence apparatus. They certainly hoped for resurgent Gaullism. And they worked to maintain contact with the General.

For some time, Moscow has been wishing that a Gaullist movement would destroy the Fourth Republic. The desire is predicated on the belief that de Gaulle would not succeed in straightening out his country's basic problems and would, at the same time, destroy France's NATO ties. Then, the Kremlin prays, a popular-front government could take over.

Vinogradov therefore took pains to assure de Gaulle that his Government believes in the tradition of French-Russian amity, in the cooling of Communism's ideological fire, and in Soviet insistence on a peace which renders military alliances unnecessary.

Gajewski's aims were different. He also stressed old ties with France. He hopes de Gaulle will back Polish claims to the new frontier with Germany.

These four envoys forecast coming events with clarity. And, furthermore, the Communist Ambassadors took pains to establish warm relationships—at least as warm as the disdainful General will permit.

Although testy, impatient, and authoritarian, Charles de Gaulle is no dictator. There is every reason to believe his assurances on this point. He has a profound, mystical belief that he not only represents the best in French tradition but that he is France. This is difficult for Americans to comprehend. But it is essential to a true understanding of the General's personality.

He has now staged the most remarkable political comeback in modern history, even more remarkable than that of Winston Churchill in 1940. It is too early to judge the success of de Gaulle's second experiment in statecraft. But it is not too early to measure the man.

He is not easy to know nor given to intimacies. Nevertheless, this writer has had the privilege of talking with him many times over the years. The following assessment, without violating confidences, is based on these conversations.

De Gaulle happens to be one of his country's superior literary stylists. He refuses to dictate. It is impossible by that method, he says, to "compose" a book. This sense of form is deeply imbued in the towering General. When reminded that Churchill writes with the aid of secretaries, he observes: "That is evident, Churchill has never properly *composed* a book," a very Gallic view.

Such niceties apart, de Gaulle's place in history is no more founded on artistic talent than is Churchill's. It is founded upon a talent for leadership, suited to his own nation, and a feeling for destiny.

After Stalin's death, de Gaulle remarked: "The age of giants is over. Giants can do nothing now. Churchill is the only survivor; and he can do nothing. Roosevelt is dead. Stalin died—too late. This is the epoch of Malenkov, Fanfani and Queuille." De Gaulle considered that the brief rule of these three Premiers in Russia, Italy, and France typified an era of mediocrity. In 1956 he further developed this theory:

"Nowhere in the world does any government or any statesman seem to know what they want. Their only policy is to react to events. This is not a policy. Nowhere do the leaders know what they wish. Things have taken control. Events are leading men.

"We need responsible men in power. Small men cannot answer to the responsibilities of the world. Small men cannot handle great events. Great circumstances bring forth great men. Only during crises do nations throw up giants." It was crisis that brought back de Gaulle.

What dominates the General's belief in his own and his country's role is a feeling that France merits a special "grandeur," one of his favorite words. He maintains that this land is accustomed to splendid traditions. Not too many years ago it was a massive power, like contemporary America. Consequently Frenchmen are used to glory and prestige. "They have the habit of thinking in terms of French grandeur. And there is no French grandeur."

Nor was France likely to achieve grandeur without a change of direction, de Gaulle thought, because under the previous regime it was "really impossible to re-establish any serious government."

He had little use for the Fourth Republic's political parties. He held that they depended upon "clienteles, not doctrines. People in the regime had good qualities and ability. But they were paralyzed and helpless."

De Gaulle scoffs at those who accuse him of dictatorial intentions. He argues that the constitutional reform he wants would establish an equilibrium among the executive, legislative, and judicial powers, as in the United States.

"Dictatorship," he says, "would be impossible under such a constitution. My enemies claim I wish to be a dictator. Yet I once had all the powers in my hands. Was I a dictator?"

Certainly the statements he has made since he took over sustain these views. Likewise, comfort may be derived from his choice of moderates to assist in the task of governing. His initial public words and his selection of advisers augur well. The final judgment will be history's.

FOUR

One-Man Democracy

June 1958

If de Gaulle is to succeed in establishing a strong state, the first thing to be done is to put the army in its place. To achieve such a strong state political counterrevolution is required.

De Gaulle is an officer by profession and by habit of thought. But he is also a firm believer in the authority of civilian government over that government's soldiery. He has a low esteem for an army's political acumen.

Nor is the French officer corps Gaullist by tradition. It was not Gaullist during World War II when the General made his initial mark on history. It was not Gaullist during the Fourth Republic. Only during the past month, thanks to the helplessness of the Republic and thanks also to conspiratorial prodding, did it swing into the Gaullist ranks.

De Gaulle himself is keenly aware of this. In a curious way he is responsible for infecting this country's army with the idea that it can take independent action. After all, it was he who suggested in 1940 that the military hierarchy should abandon France's then legal government.

Nevertheless, even in those wartime days, he never allowed officers such as General Henri Giraud to capture his Free French movement. Nor, it is plain, will he permit them to seek control of his present regime, even by indirection. "The army has no political force," he believes; nor should it.

He has paid lip service during the past few days to the role of the military in overthrowing the Fourth Republic's established system in both France and Algeria. "A determining factor," he called that role. And he has rewarded General Ely, a particular symbol of army unity, by reappointing him Chief of Staff.

But to date he has given nothing tangible to such paratrooper proconsuls as General Massu in Algeria or Colonel Thomazo in Corsica. And Massu has stated publicly his awareness that de Gaulle "came to power" as a result of the military insurrection. He has also obliquely indicated he expects Paris to pay a price.

This kind of talk has been echoed by Radio Algiers (an organization still under the local military). And it is certainly very highhanded talk, whose implications could be menacing. Will a clique of officers accept dictates from the General if and when such dictates do not come up to their expectations?

Obviously France's new boss is not a man to make deals or to bow down to threats. He believes in strong government; and this means firm authority over the army. Nor does he fancy the Right-wing political tendencies of the officer corps.

Some years ago he said to me in an authorized interview: "The French Right is very bourgeois and mistrustful. Many of them were for Pétain and therefore mistrust General de Gaulle. They have tended to live isolated among themselves."

He is, by instinct, against this Right and against its most powerful organized form of expression, the army. For this reason de Gaulle is his own Defense Minister.

Having achieved authority he must now harness the very forces that so recently have served him. For, in his own words, the fact that the army is patriotic "does not suffice for the army to wish to be the state."

General de Gaulle's pronouncements on Algeria have so far been imprecise. This, one may assume, is exactly what the General intended. It is too early to set out in detail any surgical plan for knifing the cancer that eats into France. First de Gaulle must tighten his grip on the Government and discipline restless elements. This applies especially to an army still dizzy with the success of its recent experiment in politics and to Right-wing extremists, who have discovered the thrill of conspiracy.

De Gaulle implies sympathy with the program of Algerian Europeans who demand "integration" with France. But he never mentions the word "integration." Likewise he has assumed the ministerial portfolio for Algeria himself, passing the chain of command on down through the army, which he also controls directly as Defense Minister.

In his heart de Gaulle does not approve of the formula desired by the colonists. Furthermore, he does comprehend many of the Arabs' aspirations. He must move with caution. What he eventually aspires to is some form of French commonwealth, loosely linking the mother country to an independent "association" of Morocco, Tunisia, and Algeria. But he would safeguard certain strategic bases, such as Tunisian Bizerte, which he regards as of "primordial interest" to France.

He has always recognized the reality of the Algerian Moslems' discontent. He acknowledges they suffered injustice under past French administrations. But he finds it hard to compare Algeria, which he likens to a *poussière,* or dust heap, with Tunisia and Morocco. Unlike Algeria, those former colonies had a long history of independent self-rule. And they do not now rely on a large European minority in order to build a viable society.

De Gaulle's concept of a commonwealth "association" dates back to World War II. These ideas have not yet crystallized. But obviously they tend in another direction from the announced aspirations of Soustelle and other politicians who hoped to use de Gaulle as a vehicle for arriving at their own objectives.

Consequently, even though the Premier expressed himself with glorious ambiguity, he has planted a suspicion in the extremists' minds that they have been deceived. If so, they have only deceived themselves. For the General has not wavered much in his conceptions.

What de Gaulle must now do is to calm down tempers on the Right, while simultaneously seeking to develop approaches to the nationalists. In the latter efforts he is aided by his old friendship with the Moroccan Sultan, who has much influence with the rebels, and by the fact that Tunisia's President Bourguiba and the imprisoned Algerian leader Messali Hadj have in the past publicly expressed desire to parley with de Gaulle.

The General has no particular affection for the Arabs. He claims history shows scant evidence of their cultural abilities, that even such splendid contributions as algebra and the creation of Islam's magnificent mosques resulted largely from the talents of captured Christian slaves. But de Gaulle is capable of setting aside these curious personal prejudices in the interest of reality.

He sees as reality the need for peace in Algeria and the need for a warm relationship between France and its former

North African territories. These goals can be realized only after complicated negotiations. And such negotiations must be preceded by the re-establishment of tranquillity and an atmosphere in which it is possible to replace shooting with diplomacy.

It is against this background that one must view the somewhat fuzzy outline of the Premier's initial Algerian program. So far it isn't really a program at all. It is merely a psychological dose, a kind of vague tranquilizer. It is designed to dampen the enthusiasm of extremists on both sides and to give hope of peace to the middle-of-the-road majority in both North Africa and France.

To date de Gaulle has chosen to be deliberately enigmatic about his program for internal reforms. He is still engaged in asserting authority over some of the conspiratorial factions that brought him to power but have grown too big for their boots. His first task remains to discipline the army and curb Algerian intriguers.

During his self-imposed exile from the political scene, he devoted much thought to some of France's evident weaknesses. And it is a good bet that he plans many surprises. He will probably seek to trim Communism's present strength, reduce the role of the middleman in economics, and try to weaken the influence in politics of both labor unions and capitalist organizations.

De Gaulle is not a fascist. Although he has contempt for existing parties, he has never indicated a desire to do away with them. He is disdainful of the press. Yet he revoked the censorship imposed by a previous administration. The constitutional reform he contemplates would guarantee democratic rights while establishing equilibrium among the state's executive, legislative, and judicial branches.

Nevertheless, the Communists are correct in assessing him as their special enemy. Russia may hope the General could facilitate Soviet foreign-policy aims by straining NATO. But Moscow's local stooges, the French Communists, are in for a thin time because de Gaulle regards them as "antinational."

He feels they cannot be relied upon to advocate policies truly useful to France. When he formed his stillborn movement, the Rally of the French People, in 1947, he claimed one of its objectives was to liquidate Communism in France. "Of course," he would confide to friends with grim humor, "that doesn't mean we want to shoot them all."

What he would seem to aspire to is a quiet revolution in which the administrative structure would be rendered less subject to the pressures of powerful lobbies. The fact that he has chosen several strong party politicians to help launch his reform indicates he doesn't want to crush the past order, merely to modify it.

The people of France seem to sense the rather Centralist philosophy of this approach. So far, the main currents of anti-Gaullist opposition have come from the far Right and Left, from the lunatic fascist fringe financed by wealthy European *colons* in Algeria, and from the worried Communists, who already hear a bell tolling for them.

The major question remains, however: Can the General apply the reforms he desires without warping the democratic method? Can he apply the restraints he deems necessary without, in the end, restraining democracy itself?

In terms of France's shifting political kaleidoscope, one might describe de Gaulle's aspirations as neither Right-wing nor Left-wing, but of the extreme Center. How extreme can the Center become?

Each French upheaval has its literary revolutionist. The Marquis de Condorcet played a role in 1789. Lamartine, the poet, featured the 1848 ruckus. And now, one century later, France's great novelist André Malraux returns flamboyantly to the political scene.

For several years this intellectual dynamist has been engrossed in an extraordinary series of art studies. He has been as far removed from the active diurnal stage as the man who summoned him back from his ivory tower, Charles de Gaulle. Indeed, de Gaulle's was the only ivory tower around of equal eminence.

But Malraux, like the General, is accustomed neither by instinct nor experience merely to ponder life. He has fought wars and joined movements all the way from China to Spain and occupied France. After the liberation he became de Gaulle's chief of information. Now, again in the Cabinet, he holds the modest title of Minister of State—one of several.

In fact, his assignment is infinitely more important than it sounds. He is not only a species of souped-up information minister. He is the orchestrator of the Gaullist revolution, the man whose task it is to sell it to the people.

Malraux is an astonishing, luminous figure. Pale, slender, tense, he has a natural nervous activity that has been magnified by wounds. He speaks French as rapidly as this fast-flowing language can be spoken. Yet, no matter how his tongue races, it can never catch his thoughts. When one listens to this passionate torrent, one longs for the serenely composed paragraphs of that other conversationalist, de Gaulle.

The regime which succeeds the Fourth Republic is not that Republic's legatee, seeking to execute its will, says Malraux. It is a link between old and new, a "Government of Public Safety." If it masters its problems, it will have paved the way for France's Fifth Republic.

In other words, Malraux sees this administration as transitory, a steppingstone toward the future. "The Fourth Republic died as a consequence of Dienbienphu and the bombing of Sakiet," he says. "Now we must save France and reform her."

To do this, Malraux says, de Gaulle has assembled an informal brain trust to accomplish swiftly objectives similar to those of the New Deal period in the U.S. Ultimately a new constitution, in many respects like that of the United States, will be presented for public approval.

De Gaulle confers continually with changing committees of ministers and experts, tackling specific matters. Among the very first are housing and scientific research. Plans are being drafted to build lodging in the Paris region for one million people. Unprecedented tax benefits will favor creation of private foundations for science. These will be announced within two months.

But the most dramatic need, as Malraux sees it, is to capitalize on the sudden spirit of "fraternization" between Moslems and Europeans in Algeria and to end the rebellion. He promises that "Islamic battalions," fighting for France, will go into battle against the insurgents "before July 14." Once the insurrection has been tranquilized, there will be a novel solution "because old-fashioned colonialism is over."

Malraux admits that de Gaulle must save the country from extremes of both Right and Left. To reinvigorate democracy, he argues, it is necessary to diminish Communism's influence. How will the Communists be cut down? Malraux smiles. "I will do it," says this former Left-winger. "But I won't talk about it. Communism destroys democracy. Democracy can also destroy Communism."

Malraux insists that this interim regime, brought to power legally but on the curling edge of chaos, has revolutionary intentions but intends to achieve them in nonrevolutionary ways. He says: "We will propose a change of institutions. But we don't desire brutal rupture with the past. The changes must be accomplished in peace."

These ambitions are huge—to make of France a great modern country in one dizzy rush of speed. And the atmosphere in the office of Malraux, who sees the prospect with poetic vision, is kinetic. For he is *metteur en scène* of a revolutionary spectacle, devoting all his immense energy to this immense labor. "Now," he observes, "is not a time for literature."

The fortress most menaced by General de Gaulle is a squat stone building situated on the verge of Paris's financial district. Perhaps aware of an incongruous location, it is carefully fitted with heavy doors and interior barriers of wire network. This sullen piece of architecture is headquarters for France's Communist party.

Inside the ponderous portal, cheerful, burly individuals chat affably, using the familiar *tutoyer* verb form with which party members, high and low, address each other. Upstairs, on the third floor, in a plain office featuring a model locomotive, sits the man who more than any Frenchman hopes for de Gaulle's downfall.

Maurice Thorez, the fifty-eight-year-old Communist boss, is no longer the hefty miner of those days when he himself was a minister in the General's first post-liberation Government. In 1950 he suffered a bad stroke. Consequently, despite protracted medication in the Soviet Union, his right arm is paralyzed and hangs uselessly by his side. But he is still vigorous, ruddy-complected, and energetic. And he knows he is in for the fight of his life.

This battle is for double-or-nothing stakes. The Communists hope to topple de Gaulle and then to play an ever-more-leading role in any succeeding Administration. But they are aware of enormous difficulties. Gaullists like Malraux, himself once a Marxist sympathizer, say openly: "You can't talk of a democratic system when you have in its midst a powerful Communist organism."

Thorez argues that the struggle shaping up resembles the contest between fascism and democracy which blotted Europe after World War I. "Not," he says, "that we call de Gaulle a fascist. But his is a personal dictatorship. He came in by force. He is maintained in power by the military. The situation is not yet fascism; but it can lead only to fascism."

To frustrate such a development, Thorez wants all republican elements to join forces. He is sure de Gaulle intends to suppress the Communists. Therefore, he warns other parties they should have learned from the experience of Italy and Germany that their own suppression would inevitably follow.

Thorez claims to be advocating a new political tactic. He is not reverting to the popular-front formula of the past. This sought to band together only parties of the Left—Communists, Socialists, and Radicals. "Now," he says, "we want a broader program—co-operation with *all* true republicans.

This is a vaster concept. It is based on all democrats. We want union of every democratic force, regardless of party." Thorez is sponsoring throughout France Committees for the Defense of the Republic. He claims thousands of these already exist. But the Government is countering swiftly in an effort to win mass backing by housing and tax reforms.

If they feel menaced, will the Communists fight to protect themselves? Thorez says the party has no paramilitary organization. Yet he adds cryptically: "We count on the masses, on the Republican Committee of Defense. They will find arms if necessary. Our *maquis* had no arms when they were first formed during the war. They found them. We will find them again if necessary. We have knowledge of military affairs. We are all soldiers. We know how to fight."

Why did the Communists not fight to block de Gaulle's accession? "We did not attempt violence," says Thorez, "because we didn't want to give him the argument that the Communists were seeking a *Putsch*. We did not wish to lend credence to such calumny."

To date the party doesn't seem to be succeeding any too brilliantly in attracting behind its leadership other anti-Gaullist elements. Therefore, the Communists face increasing isolation. Will they be able to muster popular support should they decide to fight for their existence? Today this seems unlikely.

French Communism has always been infinitely more popular at the polls than as a disciplined, coherent force. It has benefited heavily from the protest votes of malcontents. But the number of reliable party militants is relatively small.

And the backing of fellow-travelers was sharply hit by Moscow's sudden shift back to Stalinist brutality. The Kremlin seems almost as intent upon isolating the French Communists as General de Gaulle himself.

If the Gaullist revolution has accomplished nothing else so far it has at least laid bare the myth of French Communist might. Throughout the postwar era the party of Thorez and Jacques Duclos has been a powerful factor. Together with its Italian counterpart, it has been advertised by Moscow and feared by Western capitals as an immensely dangerous fifth column capable, under critical circumstances, of destroying NATO from within.

This legend has been believed by virtually everyone, including the Communists themselves. Yet, when crisis came and the Fourth Republic crumbled, the Marxist machine showed not the slightest sign of fight. It called for strikes that didn't materialize. It spoke of "action" which never came. Its exhortations to the working class met dull indifference.

Some observers speculate that the Kremlin sent secret orders to avoid truculence toward de Gaulle until his foreign policy had assumed clear shape. Others surmise that Thorez and Duclos are so confident the new regime will fail that they can afford to bide their time in anticipation of a new moment of political opportunity next autumn. But if the new Gaullist regime can maintain its present momentum and can win any real labor support, French Communism will sicken.

July 1958

Today is the national holiday of America's oldest ally, France. On July 14, 1789, a howling mob stormed the Bastille. That grim bastion was no longer of particular importance either as fortress or prison. But its destruction became the symbol of revolution, a revolution which, even in its first phase, took a long time to get started and which, after 169 years, is really not yet finished.

The current aspect of this continuing process which has zigzagged through history is represented by de Gaulle, once again in the seat of power. His ideas are not revolutionary in any ideological or economic sense. They are nationalistic. They seek to recapture for his country a greater role in world affairs. In the French tradition de Gaulle stems more from Bonaparte than Robespierre.

He himself has a deep sense of this persistence of history. He feels that neither the great revolution nor any other significant change in his country has yet been completed. Two years ago he said to me: "In France nothing is ever definitive, not even impotence." But it is that "impotence" which so unhappily marked the Fourth Republic that he is now out to erase.

Last February 20, only a few weeks before that same Fourth Republic was toppled by one of the oddest aspects of the continuing revolution, de Gaulle told me: "If I were in power, without this type of regime, something would be done." He is now in power. And movement is at last perceptible upon what had for long been a static political scene.

The Premier is obsessed by the idea that France is still fated to pay off past debts, debts going all the way back to the 1870 Prussian war. The nation admittedly gave an appearance of having regained vigor by 1914. But this, he feels, was a deception. Only now are the results of that deception fully evident.

Obviously Paris's present nuclear policy is partly designed to awaken his compatriots. If France can explode its own atomic bomb, regardless of strategic realities, it will give the population a "great power" feeling.

The Premier has never been known as a particularly cheerful optimist. For long he has forecast a nervous international situation—one which "will not be gay" over the coming years. Even at the height of Khrushchev's New Look policy he was saying: "There will be coexistence; but it will not be sincere. There will be exchanges of visits, of ballets, of football teams and sporting groups. During that time the Russians will continue to develop economically and to progress.

"They will progress farther in the Arab world. But I think they will have their own psychological difficulties and also political difficulties with the slave peoples—Poland, Hungary, the satellites. And the West will make its own coexistence—but without satisfaction, without a policy. And Europe will vegetate."

These previsions have proved remarkably accurate. But now that de Gaulle is again a singularly important world factor, he is determined that at least France shall no longer vegetate. A perhaps illogical search for glory, for power, for sops to national pride may feature this resolve. But presumably the General reckons such may prove a small price to pay for success in his efforts to restore the confidence and spirit of a revolution begun at the Bastille's walls.

October 1958

The question lingers in skeptics' minds: After de Gaulle, what?

The new Constitution is tailored to the General's towering

measurements. It seeks to reconcile the need for effective executive authority, lacking under four previous republics, with a keen republican tradition. The balancing factor is that, under circumstances he may determine virtually alone, the new French President can assume all real powers of the state.

De Gaulle will be that President for the next seven years —provided he lives that long. And de Gaulle has proved he has no dictatorial aspirations. But can a lesser man, chosen to succeed him, exercise similar restraint with similar responsibilities?

The French are willing to gamble on the answer although they recognize weaknesses in the new legal structure. It contains obstacles against adapting itself to altered conditions. It is precise, in contrast to the unwritten British Constitution, and is almost impossible to amend, unlike the American Constitution. There is no apparent safety valve.

But nobody, as the French discovered, has yet devised a way of legislating against tyranny. De Gaulle has pledged his own honor and integrity that, under him, there shall be no absolutist trend. The people of France have faith in this honor and integrity.

Nevertheless, three massive questions persist as the Fifth Republic sets its course. The first is Algeria. Is de Gaulle's prestige, now at a zenith, sufficient to terminate the war?

The second is the army. The General has contempt for political judgments by the military. But can he curb that instrument which, by implied blackmail, brought him back to power?

And the third is Communism. Will de Gaulle consolidate

his victory and prevent the Communists from weakening the Fifth Republic as they did the Fourth?

Throughout history armies have attempted to play politics. Both in imperial Rome and in Byzantium it was the army that generally acted as emperor-maker and emperor-breaker. The army, or various of its elements, helped disintegrate Ottoman Turkey. In pre-Hitler Germany the army influenced basic policy.

Such intrusion into civilian affairs has not been usual for the French military establishment. This is because France depends primarily on conscripts for defense. Career cadres have traditionally been of secondary importance.

But when the weak Fourth Republic fought in Indochina it never dared draft ordinary citizens for this unpopular war. Consequently the role of the professional soldiery within the state began to change.

A tightly knit professional corps emerged. It was not merely an *armée de métier* such as de Gaulle advocated in his early writings. It developed into a disciplined element to be reckoned with as a potential factor in nonmilitary facets of French life.

Furthermore, this was a disillusioned factor which felt keenly its defeats in the Vietnamese jungles. As it transferred to Algeria for another antiguerrilla operation, its officers studied the doctrines of their enemies.

They read Lenin and Mao Tse-tung, rejecting Communist theory but adopting many of its action methods. They learned the importance of penetrating civilian masses, the value of indoctrination courses, the art of propaganda.

All this gave the army, as an entity, ideas it had never previously entertained. Last May, for the first time, this newly shaped force became an influence in France's political destiny. By allying itself with the discontented European colonists, or *colons,* of Algeria, it managed to overthrow the Fourth Republic and install de Gaulle.

The army infiltrated political life. Its agents assumed positions in the revolutionary committees and propaganda apparatus that gained authority in Algeria. Thus the army, almost without knowing it, tasted power.

The army now realizes it is able to play a dominant role. General Ely, its Inspector General and Chief of General Staff, has written a profoundly interesting analysis of this situation.

He admits the influence on the army of the years spent in "revolutionary war." He recognizes that the army has made a "spectacular return" into "French internal life." He describes the army as "a democratic being" with its own "social character" which constitutes an "element of wisdom."

What is this "wisdom"? Ely calls for a "cult of action." He says civilizations die when they "renounce" action. Now, under de Gaulle, he writes that the army executes government policy without pondering alternatives or discussing means of application. And the army, he insists, will always keep its place when there is "strong government" and it feels itself commanded.

But what if the army decides the Government isn't "strong" enough? Ely does not pose this question. But de Gaulle quite evidently does.

That is the meaning of his abrupt order to General Salan, the military and civilian commander in Algeria. De Gaulle not only told the army to prepare for honest elections there. He commanded its officers to get out of politics. He wrote: "The moment has come . . . for the military to stop taking part in any organization which has a political character."

From the start de Gaulle saw that the strong civilian executive he desires must curb the military or become its creature. When the popular referendum ended in his astonishing victory, he began the battle necessary to the creation of a renovated and enduring government. So far he has played the game skillfully. But he must win it totally if he is to restore vigor to French republicanism.

During his five months of regained power General de Gaulle has put on the most dazzling virtuoso performance since another Frenchman, called Blondin, walked across Niagara Falls on a tightrope just ninety-nine years ago.

France these days is a historical phenomenon. One might call it a one-man democracy. For every major decision currently taken by its Government is taken by the astonishing, complex mystic now in authority's seat.

And even the most jaded veterans of that intricate game of musical chairs indulged in by politicians of the Fourth Republic are unstinted in admiration of the skill so far shown by a man they had accounted awkward and uncompromising.

Prior to the September referendum most of de Gaulle's advisers predicted he would be approved by 65 to 70 per cent of the voters. The General himself forecast 72 per cent. His actual triumph was by 80 per cent. And were another poll to be held today, his victory would be more sweeping.

De Gaulle is using his unexpected psychological momentum with maximum efficiency. During one brief week he took two steps so audacious that any other French Premier, had he ventured either of them, would have been blasted from office. But any consequent whimpers of discontent were drowned by thunderous applause.

The first thing he did was to re-establish governmental control over the military and to order the army out of politics. Revolutionary Committees of Public Safety in Algeria dissolved in confusion. The General followed this up by offering to deal directly with Algerian rebel leaders to terminate the dreary civil war.

It is worth analyzing the methods employed in this fascinating series of maneuvers. With little fanfare de Gaulle put an end to what has been called the "paratrooper period." This period existed from the moment the army decided on its own last February to bomb a Tunisian village until after it joined with Right-wing revolutionists to project the General into power.

De Gaulle placed in positions of authority officers he considered loyal to him, among them General Jean Gilles, General André Zeller, and General Edmond Jouhaud. He transferred such military hotheads as Colonel Roger Trinquier, Colonel Louis Ducasse, and Colonel Thomazo.

When these potential fomenters of trouble had been shifted, de Gaulle removed the armed forces totally from the realm of political conspiracy into which certain officers had entered with delight.

While the military was being separated from civilian affairs, de Gaulle acted on another front. He thwarted an attempt by Right-wing politicians to join in a new party pretending to express his views. He simply refused permission for any group to appropriate his name.

While ultraconservative opposition therefore remained F.L.N. rebels to come to Paris and negotiate a cease-fire. What will come of his offer cannot yet be foreseen. There are indications he had prepared for it by sending discreet hints to the insurrectionist chiefs.

The majority of Frenchmen is impressed. The Right is dazed. The Communists are on the run. And Liberal opponents of the General have begrudgingly commenced to say kind words.

The first important international consequence of de Gaulle's return to power has been a French demand for greater influence in NATO.

De Gaulle has been bearish about the coalition from the start.

In 1949, when the North Atlantic Treaty was signed, he claimed it gave an insufficient military role to France. He asserted it deprived the French of the initiative they required to build their own defense. Two years later he was complaining that France held insufficient commands and was not called upon to contribute enough divisions. He proposed forty French divisions, half ready and half on an eight-day reserve basis.

By 1955 de Gaulle was saying that neither the United Nations nor NATO had much meaning. The following year he thought NATO only existed when Russia threatened; that with soft winds from the Kremlin it would disintegrate. The atomic bomb, he told friends, had big value. But NATO—pooh—what value had that?

In 1957 he began to consider the possibility of French withdrawal from NATO unless it was greatly modified. He considered that France had become an American satellite. Some months ago he held the opinion that France should get out of the alliance because it was "against" his country's "interest and independence."

He argued that if Russia bombed France, America would react only by protests to the U.N.; it would not fight unless directly attacked. He thought NATO was weakening French resolve and gradually easing France out of Algeria and the Tunisian base of Bizerte.

De Gaulle called NATO "no longer an alliance but a subordination." He insisted that France must regain more freedom of action. He still dreams of *"une grandeur Française."* This great France could not, he feels, accept American superiority in allied commands or obligations. He regards the United States, governmentally, as a great friend of France although he thinks the American and French people share a mutual disdain. But he is worried about the extent of his nation's reliance upon its transatlantic ally for military protection.

In effect, what Paris wants is a political committee similar to the military standing group that directs alliance strategy from Washington. The latter includes representatives from France, the United States, and Britain. The former does not exist.

To qualify for recognition as one of the three North Atlantic great powers, Paris has already taken certain steps. It wants American nuclear arms, but since they cannot at present be provided, it is joining the "atomic club" by starting manufacture of nuclear weapons, although they will be rudimentary and expensive. And, while promising to make more vital NATO contributions, it asks larger command responsibilities in return.

The problem for France as a nation with world-wide interests is philosophically the same as for the United States and Britain. Each would like to commit the other precisely within the specified NATO area. But they wish an individually free hand elsewhere as well as a share in everybody else's over-all strategy outside North Atlantic pact boundaries. Neither the United States nor Britain acknowledges the right of even close partners to prejudge their actions in, for example, Asia.

This puzzle is comprehensible and totally unresolved. It concerns the dichotomy of any global power's policy within a coalition and without. Paris now desires at least to share in this dichotomy on an equal basis with Washington and London.

So far neither America nor Britain is disposed to establish a Big Three governing committee to co-ordinate world policy. The small allies are suspicious and resentful. And Germany, which has seen its own importance grow within the European power balance, hasn't the slightest wish to relinquish this relative prestige to Gaullist France.

FIVE

The Age of Giants?

November 1958

De Gaulle makes no secret of his mistrust for military judgments in the realm of politics and his distaste for all reactionary elements. For many weeks he has been reasserting governmental control over army hotheads.

Until a fortnight ago it seemed as if he had succeeded brilliantly. But it is now apparent that the antidemocratic coalition of officers and politicians is re-forming on what might be called a guerrilla basis. And this political guerrilla has managed to embarrass de Gaulle by ruining his efforts to stage a truly representative election in Algeria.

Diehard officers in Algeria seem to be combining the methods learned in Indochina with a new form of political warfare against the Gaullist regime's expressed ideals. Broken in terms of open opposition to the Paris Government, the diehards have re-formed on a kind of commando basis. And on this basis they have subverted the General's policy by discouraging most European liberals and Moslem nationalists from standing for Parliament. In this they were paradoxically aided by the rebel F.L.N., which threatened to murder many Moslem candidates because it wishes to insure that only it can speak for Algerian nationalism. The Algerian electoral ticket is made up largely of reactionaries and their Mohammedan stooges.

Furthermore, several officers who had been active in politics and were therefore transferred from Algeria are now standing as Parliamentary candidates in France. These include such antidemocratic toughs as Colonel Jean Thomazo, who captured Corsica for the insurrection that destroyed the Fourth Republic.

Having been thwarted in overt attempts to dictate policy, Right-wing officers are now trying to penetrate the Government and influence it from within. One of them says: "We will not be had this time. We were opposed to Algerian elections because we knew they would be harmful and impossible. But, if it is absolutely necessary to have Deputies from there, we won't elect men who might shoot us in the back or sell us out."

The army diehards have managed to frustrate de Gaulle's promise of free democratic expression in Algeria. The General had hoped such expression would bring to the fore genuine nationalists with whom he could negotiate.

Hopes of ending the rebellion have thus been set back by the two groups doing the shooting. To say that the General is angry would be an understatement. For the first time since his tidal wave of popularity began, the momentum of his drive to reform France is faltering. But de Gaulle is stubborn and determined. It is certain he will permit neither the army nor any of its elements to sabotage his program.

Once he said to me, and there is no reason to suspect he has changed his mind: "The army in France has no political force. It is, of course, always for order and *la Patrie*. It is also always against weak governments.

"But that does not suffice for the army to wish to be the state. No revolution in French history was ever made by the army. The eighteenth-century revolution was made by the bourgeoisie. The people made Bonaparte. Not even Pétain was made by the army—that was Parliament. And de Gaulle was not made by the army."

February 1959

Today there is no doubt that de Gaulle himself holds the real power. The Elysée Palace, traditional residence of Presidents, has for the first time become France's operational center. The same dapper policemen in dark-blue capes, the same Republican Guards, wearing red-plumed shakos, patrol the French White House. The same discreet flunkeys, wearing their chains of office, glide through its high-ceilinged rooms.

But the aura is different. A vast and complex staff has replaced the leisurely handful that served previous Presidents. Cabinet Ministers bustle in and out. Functionally, the Presidency has altered.

Policy is today set by the President. In this sense, if in none other, a gigantic era has set in. France is dominated by a single man's personality. The future will weigh its impact.

He has been President for but a few weeks, although during preceding months he held unprecedented powers. His initial task was to calm the convulsion that accomplished his return. Now he has set himself grim, long-range tasks.

De Gaulle aspires to regain France's position as Europe's fulcrum. And he covets recognition for France as one, with Britain and the United States, of the three free world powers with global obligations.

He wants to re-create the equilibrium of France itself and make his nation eligible for the "grandeur" he considers its due. This requires restoration of internal economic and political balance and, above all, settlement of the Algerian war that drains French wealth and energy.

. . .

The only army that has been constantly at war for twenty years is that of France. During two decades it has fought in Europe, Asia, and Africa, for the most part in lost causes.

The French army, which cherishes a proud tradition, feels condemned to fight at a disadvantage. In 1904 it was overwhelmed because the Third Republic failed to prepare it for modern conflicts. It had inadequate weapons and an archaic strategy. Under the Fourth Republic it was defeated in Indochina when a series of weak Paris Governments, fearing even to call that bloody struggle "war," failed to mobilize and depended on professional officers and mercenaries.

Likewise, under the Fourth Republic, an insurrection in Algeria gained ground. This latest episode in France's effort to survive as a first-class power continues under the Fifth Republic without significant change.

During its bitter struggles the French army experienced immense psychological strains. Unwilling to blame itself for defeats caused, according to the military, by feeble leadership in Paris, the army became a restless political force. In World War II it had already learned to choose—between Pétain and de Gaulle. It had to ponder when a particular oath of allegiance might no longer be deemed binding.

Army morale has been somewhat re-established by de Gaulle's assumption of strong central power. But the army is not entirely happy. It used to blame its difficulties on "politics." Today it blames "diplomacy."

General Jacques Massu, the burly paratrooper who commands the key Algerian region, is renowned as the leading figure of last spring's *Putsch*. He boasts a reputation for toughness which endears him to most French Algerians and earns him the hatred of Moslem nationalists. A tall man with short-cut hair, enormous ears and nose, and a prognathous jaw, Massu resembles his name, which, in French, means "club." He uses clublike methods.

He denies that he employs torture to extract information from terrorists, but he adds, menacingly: "We do use tough interrogation. One gets nowhere with politeness. However, I have given orders that no man's physical or moral integrity shall be harmed; no physical or moral traces may be left. I defend Western civilization. I cannot employ totalitarian methods. Nevertheless we must adapt ourselves to subversive war." Massu contends that to defeat guerrillas it is necessary first to surround them, then to annihilate them. This, he says, can be locally achieved by ground and air envelopment. But the diplomatic task is to isolate the insurgents from their supply bases in Tunisia and Morocco.

"In the end," Massu observes ruefully, "it is diplomacy that counts. A Greek Communist rebellion was crushed only when Greece's border was closed. Here we have the same problem. The F.L.N. depends upon its bases in Tunisia and Morocco. It is a question of diplomacy."

Defensive lines have been constructed to hinder such assistance from abroad. But their effectiveness is only partial. Regardless of steady battlefield losses, the rebels maintain an almost constant fighting strength.

Here, as in Indochina, there is no juridically declared war. French soldiers are fighting Algerian partisans for a philosophical purpose of making them unwilling citizens of France. Thus, in its twentieth year of almost uninterrupted combat, a gallant army finds itself fighting with no traditionally definable cause and against an enemy able always to seek rescue in sympathetic, neighboring lands.

The Test: De Gaulle and Algeria

March 1959

Now that Cyprus has been tranquilized there is only one major active battle front in the world—Algeria. Elsewhere there are cold wars, minor military operations, and police actions. But the Algerian war is both extensive and hot.

Supplied from bases in Tunisia and Morocco, some 30,-000 disciplined guerrillas are immobilizing most of France's armed striking power.

Allied defenses in Europe are, as a result, denuded of their best French divisions. And inflamed Arab nationalism, sympathizing with the Algerian rebels, refuses to consider accommodations with the West that might shore up our position in the Middle East.

At present both the French and the rebels seem to be pursuing a policy of strategic stalemate. About 400,000 well-equipped and beautifully conditioned French soldiers find themselves unable to isolate and crush the guerrillas, who fight in small units and are refurbished from abroad. But the guerrillas, on the other hand, are not strong enough to oust the French.

Paris cannot envision any peace formula that might abandon a minority of 1,000,000 Frenchmen to domination by 9,000,000 Moslems.

It places much future hope in a massive program of social and economic reform. This is designed to improve living standards and win over Algerian Moslems who are fed up with terror and brutal rebel exactions, thus depriving the guerrillas of essential popular support.

This program requires time before results can show. Therefore, French military strategy seeks to gain time. And time is also important to the rebels. They know they cannot expel France's powerful military establishment. They feel, however, they may eventually weaken French resolve by threatening an economy burdened with enormous war costs.

But this prospect of indefinite bloodshed contains unpredictable dangers. How long will the French army be content to take losses in a war that promises no real victory? This same army was up to the ears in last May's plot against the Fourth Republic.

Prior to that *coup d'état,* certain officers talked of reconquering Morocco and Tunisia, where there are still strong French garrisons, to destroy the guerrillas' safe havens. There is no such talk today. The army respects de Gaulle's firmness. It previously revolted not against the authority of Paris but against its lack of authority. However, if the new authority fails to produce Algerian peace, no one can guarantee that an army which has tasted political conspiracy will forever remain quiescent.

The French argue that a pro-French settlement is necessary for all NATO. They contend that abandonment of Algeria would erode the alliance's heart by provoking civil war in France and would swing all North Africa into the enemy camp.

In seeking such settlement, there has been a lamentable lack of originality. Obviously, as in Cyprus, past mottoes must be abandoned. French "integration" must join Greek *"enosis"* in history's scrap basket. In both instances slogans have been superseded by events or rendered impossible by realities.

Nevertheless, it is surely not beyond diplomatic imagination to conceive of new approaches. Partition, as we learned in India and Palestine, is an unsatisfactory solution. But de Gaulle's French Community concept contains great flexibility. Can it not produce a special Algerian formula?

The chances of outright military settlement are slim. No Tunisian or Moroccan Government can refuse to aid the rebels and survive. Civilized France cannot invade Tunisia and Morocco.

The ultimate settlement must be political. Cannot some of the ingenuity that rescued Cyprus from disaster now be applied to the Algerian war? It is time for new approaches. The strategy of stalemate is risky in a world on the edge of holocaust.

Monsieur D., who owns a farm in Algeria's war-ravaged hinterland called the bled, requests that his identity be obscured because: "If the *fellaghas,* the rebels, learn that I've been talking, I will be *égorgé.*" *Egorgé* is a common word in the bled. It means to have one's throat cut.

On the borders of what he calls No Man's Land, Monsieur D. produces olive oil, grain, tobacco, and wine on some two hundred acres. All civilians have been evacuated from the mountain massif opposite and the road is barred. For that is a hunting ground of the *fellaghas* and France's army.

The only French house hereabouts that has not been burned is that of Monsieur D. From a rise he points: "See, there; burned. Over there, burned and the vineyards cut. And there, burned; the owner was *égorgé.* In that field my neighbor was *égorgé* while he was working, just two years ago. Last week an officer was shot on this slope. That farm was burned one Sunday while the *patron* played at bowls. There is my nephew's farm, burned. And we have been here since 1858."

Monsieur D.'s blue eyes water slightly behind their spectacles. "One must defend one's self," he says. "This is my country and I am part of it just like the trees and rocks. I will never quit. Sometimes I shake in my boots but I won't pull down the flag."

The wall around Monsieur D.'s home is ringed with barbed-wire coils and the windows are barred and netted against grenades, their lower halves shielded by sheet steel or wooden boxes packed with earth. Inside, next to a sandbag barrier, is a siren to summon emergency aid. The roof is fortified and equipped with a homemade mortar. Everywhere are caches of bombs, revolvers, rifles, shotguns, ammunition. "I'll fight from here," Monsieur D. explains, designating an intricate array of barbed wire running beneath a lemon tree and by a rosebush, "while the women shelter in my cellar redoubt."

Regarding his visitor, Monsieur D. inquires: "Where is your gun? Here, take this." Exposing his own Parabellum in its shoulder holster, he reaches behind some books and draws out another automatic. He continues: "Of course, if the moment comes, I'll have to fight alone. My wife is useless with a weapon. The children are at boarding school. And you see our Moslem workers in the yard? I will never give them arms.

"But I help them and I understand them. It's a lie to say the natives hate the French. However, they are afraid. They have their relatives with the *fellaghas*. They are scared to warn me but they sometimes say: 'Hey, thou! Don't go down by the stream today.' Or 'Old man, better not drive around this afternoon.' "

In the gathering dusk Madame D. closes doors and shutters while her husband, placing his pistol on the mantelpiece, relaxes with an *apéritif*. His favorite cat sits purring upon his head. A taut, weather-beaten man, Monsieur D., with long nose and ruddy complexion; in knickerbockers, corduroys, and khaki shirt, he resembles the Gallic version of a Grant Wood portrait.

"Alors," says he, "this time the army won't desert us. They can't admit their blood has run in vain. But Paris, what does Paris know? De Gaulle is strong and we respect him, but he does not love us.

"Some call us oppressors, feudal lords, exploiters. *Patati, patata;* this is false. My Moslems like me, but they are archaic and they need a tribal leader, me. They are like tractors or like donkeys. You must mount to make them work. Otherwise they do nothing. They don't plant trees; they cut them; they let their goats devour saplings and move on.

"We are the pioneers who understand and made this country. Our bones are in its cemeteries. In France they do things the old way, but here we are new men, not chained to the past. We're not politicians; we only want to stay, work hard, and *vive la France.*" Monsieur D. regards his pretty wife. She says: "We shall live here. Or we'll die here."

Algeria's Bled, that lovely countryside so scarred by terror, is filled with modest peasant huts called *gourbis.* Here dwell the Moslems, both Berber Kabyles and Arabs, who are the flotsam of war between the French and rebel Nationalists.

Isolated on the edge of fear, Brahim's *gourbi* is considered relatively prosperous. But to one side, on a peak, is a French military post. Equidistant, on another side, is a *harka* detachment, the French-officered native home guard. And opposite, on the mountain, are hidden insurgents. When evening draws about, the whisper of agents starts: French demanding information; guerrillas exacting food and money.

Brahim's *gourbi* is situated on a slope whose zigzag path, in the heavy rainstorm, is a concatenation of puddles. The tiled roof leaks upon the earthen floor where Brahim and his brother, Moussa, squat beside their visitors upon straw mats.

Moussa's unveiled, bloomered wife searches beneath the bed, where precious things are stored, for coffee and sugar. Two barefooted lads and a baby girl pad in through a room that serves jointly as kitchen and as byre for three dwarf cows that must, at all cost, be kept warm. Altogether, inhabited by innumerable friends and relatives, there are four rooms set around an open central court where bedraggled sheep and chickens shelter beneath an eave.

"No," says Brahim, the household's head, "life is not easy for us now." He speaks in Arabic, pausing for interpretation. "We have food—wheat and barley for couscous and bread" (the flat, unleavened, stone-baked loaves). "We have eggs, chick-peas, turnips, sour milk. We cannot buy beans; they are too expensive. But we have coffee and some sugar. On feast days we eat meat."

The women bring in a battered tray, two cups and spoons, a few sugar lumps. Brahim pours, sweetens, stirs, and serves thick Arab coffee. He gravely accepts a cigarette, displaying confidence because the *fellaghas* have forbidden this luxury to Moslems.

"But how are we to live?" asks Brahim. "Sometimes the *moudjahids* come down the mountains." Here the Algerians call the *fellagha* rebels *moudjahids,* fighters for the sacred cause. "When they come they ask for food and money. If we do not give?" Brahim draws his hand across his throat.

"Then the French or *harkis* come and ask us questions. And if we tell?" In heavily accented French he repeats the dreadful byword of the Bled, *"Egorgé,"* the cut throat, *"égorgé* by the *moudjahids."*

Dusk is settling, ominous and heavy. Moussa lights a rusty kerosene lamp, hanging it from a peg in the thick, clay wall. "What does everyone want of us?" asks Brahim. "The *moudjahids* say we are Algerians and we must help them. The French say we are French.

"We have kinsmen in the *moudjahids* and kinsmen in the *harkas.* When the *moudjahids* have been around, the officer comes to ask us questions. And when the officer has gone, the *moudjahids* return. The French say we will be like them. But how does one change? If you put the curling greyhound's tail within a rifle barrel it still curls when you pull it out.

"I love and admire the *moudjahids,* my cousins. They tell us that the French must go. But what is my quarrel with the French? I work in the vineyard of a Frenchman who is as my grandfather. My son goes to their school down in the village."

He murmurs something to the older boy in Arabic. The youngster produces an illustrated reader. He is eleven and has had four years of schooling. He reads in awkward French: "These buildings, made possible by a continually expanding output of cement . . ." Brahim observes him proudly, comprehending nothing.

"Nobody leaves us alone," says Brahim. "The price of beans is rising. Everyone tells me something different. My people are afraid. May God take care of us," he adds without conviction.

It is late. With immaculate courtesy Brahim draws his ragged coat about him, settles his little turban against the wind, and escorts his callers out into the night. He stares across the valley at the mountain's shadow. "May God take care of us," he says again uncertainly, looking into the dark for God.

From the air an observer would discern nothing but pastoral landscape: hills divided by creek beds and grazing grounds; rocks and scrub thickets with, every here and there, tree groves such as the one beneath which these guerrillas are located. During daylight little movement can be noticed: the wheeling of birds, the occasional scurrying of rodents. It is only at night that the rebels issue forth.

These rebels, who call themselves *moudjahids,* fighters for the sacred cause, and who are known as *fellaghas,* or bandits, by the French, constitute the Algerian Army of National Liberation, the A.L.N., an experienced partisan force. Since 1954 France has sought unsuccessfully to crush it. But, like the famous Hydra of the Lernaean swamp, two heads spring up for every one sliced off.

These hardy youths, capable of forty-mile marches, appear well trained, well officered, and adequately equipped. Their khaki uniforms, with visored caps and rubber-soled shoes, derive from other Arab lands or seized French stores. The visitor finds items clearly originating in the Suez stockpiles left to Nasser by Britain and still labeled "Cyprus to U.K.," "Egypt to U.K.," "Malaya to U.K."

This unit is drawn from all over Algeria. One lieutenant, graduate of a French officers' academy, served France ten years as a professional. Until 1957 he retained his command, pretending to fight the A.L.N., but secretly supplying it. When informed he was about to be denounced, he deserted with all his post's equipment, thirty Algerians and thirty French captives.

A redheaded Berber from the Kabylia tells of volunteering after a French patrol slew his family. An Arab from Algiers of slightly Mongoloid countenance says his parents were killed by bombs. A medical student from Constantine took up arms following a school strike.

The most impressive tale is that of Major Azzedine, renowned among the *moudjahids* and French. Azzedine, which means "beloved of faith," is the *nom de guerre* of twenty-five-year-old Zerrari Rabah, a former factory worker whose exploits are legendary. Twice captured by the French as he lay unconscious, he boasts thirteen wounds. Now he is heading eastward to Tunisia and a European hospital to have extracted from one gnarled arm an explosive shell which, he carefully points out, is of American manufacture.

Once Azzedine escaped from prison with thirteen others, but last autumn he was retaken. By then he was sufficiently esteemed to be interviewed in the hospital by France's General Jacques Massu. "I salute you as a brave man," said Massu. "Your courage is written on your body."

Massu proposed his prisoner should return to the A.L.N. to arrange a possible cease-fire. Azzedine pretended to agree. He slipped into the mountains, came back to Algiers with false information, gathered intelligence, and then left—for good. French propagandists claimed the A.L.N. had shot him.

Azzedine, like many of these soldiers, harbors considerable rancor for the United States. A wiry, mustachioed, black-haired individual with gleaming eyes, he observes: "I have six unremoved bullets in me—all American-made. My people say we would have had peace long ago if America didn't aid France. You claim this help is for NATO and for Europe. I only know your bullets."

One way or another the future of Algeria must lie with this generation of battle-hardened partisans. It is not that they have succeeded in enlisting foreign support to equip themselves with enough mortars, mines, tommy guns, and rifles to tie up most of France's North Atlantic striking power. It is that they represent the emotional aspirations of all North Africa. This is just the latest aspect of an Arab revolt that began forty-five years ago in the Levant and has since seethed from the Indian Ocean to the Atlantic. History is with these people.

The tragic Algerian conflict could well continue for years against a resolute France. But in the end the solution must accord with the anticolonial sentiments of our age. One sergeant says: "Almost a million of us, principally civilians, have been slain. We have paid a great price for our liberty. But we thirst for human dignity and freedom. Nothing, absolutely nothing, can defeat us."

June 1959

The most extraordinary aspect of de Gaulle's comeback is that, in one year, the General has restored to France her self-respect, her international prestige, and her fiscal health without, in fact, materially restoring France. That is to say, the same essential weaknesses that eroded the Fourth Republic still erode the Fifth: cumbersome distribution, archaic taxes, and the bloody, cruel, expensive Algerian war.

De Gaulle has nevertheless shown extraordinary genius by remolding French psychology even before applying surgery to basic problems. The French people are today more proud and confident than they were a year ago. De Gaulle has given back to them a consciousness of grandeur and the *élan vital* without which the French are unable fully to exercise their genius.

De Gaulle has always mystically associated his own person with the personality of France. His whole life has been devoted to restoring French greatness, for, as he says: "France is not really herself unless in the front rank. . . . France cannot be France without greatness."

The President of the old Republic used to be a figurehead. But today de Gaulle presides over and controls Cabinet meetings; the Premier and Foreign Minister report personally to him almost daily. The Elysée Palace, France's White House, is the real seat of power. There has been a more significant organizational revolution in the Elysée than that which occurred in the White House during the early New Deal. In the sense of Franklin Roosevelt, who disliked him, de Gaulle has become both the symbol of his nation and its primary executive, strategic, and diplomatic officer.

He is thus in a position to apply concepts which even his own most competent technicians consider awkward or diplomatically risky. Against their advice, he has insisted and continues to insist on radical reform of NATO.

The mere fact that Washington does not accept his views does not deter de Gaulle. Unless the United States ultimately agrees to extend NATO's umbrella over Africa and the Red Sea area, as the General wants, and to give France a greater share of allied responsibilities, de Gaulle will remain on what is tantamount to a North Atlantic sit-down strike. He refuses to allow establishment of missile ramps on French soil or to place his air defenses under integrated command. He has pulled his Mediterranean fleet away from SHAPE. He may extricate still other French forces from present assignments if Washington refuses his demands.

De Gaulle says: We do not contemplate a change from our NATO policy. We regard NATO as necessary and France will not leave the alliance. But we will cease practicing our membership in the same way as we practiced it in the past. There are other ways. Only if there is no comprehension of our viewpoint would we be forced to take back our liberty of action; but I do not foresee this; all logic points to an accord.

Certain American officials regret this stubborn and even arrogant attitude on the part of a country the United States has been accustomed to regard as weak and dependent. But if France is today a more demanding partner, it is also an infinitely more vibrant partner.

Disagreements now persisting are capable of resolution. But they can only be resolved by direct talks with de Gaulle himself, because, governmentally speaking, he is France. And President Eisenhower alone is regarded by de Gaulle as his American peer, competent to settle prevailing arguments.

One may therefore hope that during the second year of the Gaullist renaissance the two wartime heroes may meet and negotiate a new basis for our oldest alliance. After all, de Gaulle says: "I would like to see the President. He has been my friend since always."

July 1959

Until now the principal atomic striking power placed at NATO's disposal by the United States has been composed of nine jet fighter-bomber squadrons stationed on airfields in

France. Shortly these planes will be transferred to bases in West Germany and Britain.

This move, which is highly inconvenient to the alliance's high command, was forced by General de Gaulle's wish to control the use and disposition of nuclear weapons on French territory. When it was explained to him that American law makes it impossible to grant this, he was not impressed.

This development is a piece of de Gaulle's plan to change the entire Western power relationship to suit his concepts of a grander and more prestigious France. And, to the accompaniment of much allied grumbling, his obstinacy is paying off.

Before the end of this year France will have exploded its own atom device in the Sahara. The French have already manufactured enough plutonium to make perhaps ten Hiroshima-type bombs. There is some suspicion they have delayed their experiment to produce a more modern and impressive kind of weapon.

SHAPE headquarters, the State Department, and the Pentagon have voiced private complaints about awkward and embarrassing French policy. NATO has undoubtedly been greatly inconvenienced by the forced shift of our jets and by de Gaulle's insistence on greater command privileges, an insistence given point by the removal of the Mediterranean fleet from allied control.

He has irked the British intensely by turning the European Common Market, designed to help French Continental trade, into a political association. London is furious at what it regards as its exclusion from markets on the Continental side of the Channel.

De Gaulle has even irritated his great new friends, the

Germans. He publicly stated what everybody knew but refused to admit—that the Oder-Neisse Line must be the eastern border of any reunited German state. And he is quietly attempting to achieve the removal of General Hans Speidel as NATO's army commander on the central sector.

In a fundamental sense the Western world must regard these trends favorably. France is unified; it has a stable currency, an improving economy, and a diplomatic policy that is consistent even if we find it sometimes clumsy. The French have not ceded an inch to a mixture of Soviet threats and blandishments and, while reinterpreting their own role, they have not abandoned their international commitments.

The question now is: How can de Gaulle's ambitions be reconciled to the need for inter-allied harmony?

The political gap between France and the United States is growing even if our traditional friendship remains warm and firm.

The President entertains a tolerant and understanding view of de Gaulle. When Eisenhower commanded NATO forces he invited de Gaulle to lunch. The Frenchman declined, saying that on French soil Eisenhower should come to him—even though de Gaulle was then a private citizen. A dinner meeting was finally arranged on neutral ground. But Eisenhower never bore a grudge. He sympathizes with the Frenchman's pride, arguing that it was offended by Roosevelt during the war and that, if this had given de Gaulle a complex toward America, America should make allowances because he represents France's noblest qualities.

De Gaulle, for his part, referred in his writings to Eisenhower as "this great soldier" who "felt within him the mysterious attraction which for nearly two centuries has neared his country to mine in great world crises." He spoke of him as "adroit and flexible" and marked by "wisdom." He still considers Eisenhower a friend.

This is an admirable human background for frank discussion of questions disturbing the relations of two allies.

December 1959

De Gaulle places particular emphasis on independence, but he himself admits that "independence is a term which signifies an intention, but the world being what it is—so small, so narrow, so in opposition to itself—real independence, total independence, truly belongs to no one." This accords with Eisenhower's known views. The problem is now to reconcile material discords to this essential philosophical accord.

Although endorsing de Gaulle's self-determination promise for Algeria, Washington has avoided the total support the General asks. It has so far failed to comprehend fully the peculiar psychological conditions prevailing in France. "Algeria," for de Gaulle, means something emotional as well as geopolitical. The Fifth French Republic sprang from a military revolt in Algeria. Algeria is the hope of France's economic future, thanks to recently discovered oil. Finally, Algeria is the scene of the only hot war still being fought by any NATO power. As a result French nationalism is more aroused than the nationalism of any ally.

This was explained to Eisenhower when he visited Paris in September, and de Gaulle assumed he would receive complete backing from Washington. Consequently, Paris resented the failure of the United States to support its view in the U.N. by its abstention in the second vote on Algeria and has revived a mistrust for the U.S. reflected in NATO discussions.

Diplomacy risks becoming ineffective when it seeks to endorse two foreign policies concurrently. This truism is at the root of present difficulties between France and the United States. For, in terms of both countries, dearly and intimately related, there is a tendency to seek dual objectives at contradictory moments even if their ultimate goals may ultimately rejoin.

There is no tidy solution, because inherent discords cannot be resolved. The U.S. would compose the NATO command in terms of the most effective military logic. Yet it insists on external freedom, for example, to encourage the new nationalism that now sweeps Africa and Asia.

France demands national control of its national destiny. France is reluctant to submerge this in military commands dominated by American officers. De Gaulle argues: "You are not the West; you are only part of the West."

The argument crystallizes on these twinned topics of "Algeria" and "NATO's integration." America contends it is as much in France's interest as that of any ally to recognize that Western defenses must be fully unified to be effective. The United States sees no relationship between this premise and the somewhat separate issue of French North Africa.

De Gaulle disagrees. He regards such matters from another tangent. One of his closest collaborators says: "De Gaulle is the man of the day before yesterday and the day after tomorrow." Eisenhower, on the other hand, is eminently the man of today.

Eisenhower sees a new generation of nations evolving and wishes to retain liberty of action toward them. Meanwhile, however, he considers it imperative that the West should remain efficiently bound together in defense. He insists this can only be done by sacrifice of national authority to an overall international command—not binding in terms of diplomatic policy toward non-NATO areas.

Thus, both de Gaulle and Eisenhower are attempting the impossible. Presumably each will accept what appears to be a middle-of-the-road solution. But there can be no valid agreement between the spokesman for today and the spokesman for that paradox of yesterday-and-tomorrow.

January 1960

Many Americans are genuinely puzzled by French resentment over their North African policy. They simply don't understand why such things as abstentions in U.N. votes or platitudinous communiqués on friendship with Arab states inspire furious anger in Paris.

But many Americans fail to realize what a difficult problem de Gaulle now faces in France and what a venturesome step he took by promising Algerian self-determination. Embers of rebellion still smolder among right-wing settlers in Algeria.

De Gaulle has gone a long way toward reasserting control over malcontents in the officer corps. But it is no secret that dissidents remain. Certain generals, some retired and some on active duty, maintain contact with plotters among those settlers who fear de Gaulle plans to give Algeria independence. These officers are believed to include one important general in Germany, another in Algeria, a recently retired General Staff officer, and Field Marshal Juin, militarily but not politically inactive.

The General Staff itself, under the highly regarded General Ely, is far from happy. Just before de Gaulle announced his self-determination plan, the General Staff made known its views. These were as follows: It is in the common interest of the West that France should continue to rule Algeria. If France leaves, NATO will be outflanked. Furthermore, independence is incompatible with the French state of mind and, if it is accorded, civil war might break out.

The General Staff insisted the United States must be made to accept this thesis. It claimed present American policy gives Algerian nationalists the hope of eventual success and thus sustains them even more than Soviet policy. Everything, it was argued, depends on persuading Washington to change its view.

This opinion has perforce been modified by events— above all by de Gaulle's September offer of Algerian self-determination. But its essential philosophy remains unchanged. Even General Challe, operational commander in Algeria and designated to succeed General Ely next summer, is dissatisfied.

De Gaulle has not allowed himself to be swayed. Nevertheless, both he and his civilian ministers feel the United States has shown too little comprehension of French interests in North Africa and France's developing policy in that area. A hypersensitivity exists in Paris which is difficult for foreigners to appreciate.

As long as the Algerian war continues there can be no real felicity in Franco-American relationships. The United States cannot give the French the unqualified total support they demand because this would be inconsonant with its attitude toward Afro-Asian nationalism.

But the French resent anything less than unqualified total support, which they believe their alliance merits.

General de Gaulle has decided to stake the fate of his regime on resolute pursuance of the course already fixed. This course aims at settling the Algerian question on the basis of self-determination.

It has never been any secret that landowning settlers in Algeria and certain dynamic army leaders oppose that program.

Some of the same officers who plotted two years ago to overthrow one regime, the Fourth Republic, and produce de Gaulle, have recently been plotting to overthrow another regime, de Gaulle's.

France's President is aware that at least three well-known generals have been involved in schemes. He knows that Right-wing politicians have been plotting with them. This is the reason for keeping former Premier Bidault away from Algeria and for disciplining General Massu.

De Gaulle quietly transferred from Algerian commands generals and colonels affected by the conspiratorial virus. Although more than twenty have been shifted, the replacements were often influenced by the thoughts of their predecessors.

France is par excellence the land of paradox. Thus we find today a strong Government headed by a general asserting itself against generals who were responsible for producing it. De Gaulle, himself a professional officer, fights to preserve civilian control over the armed forces. Both Government and generals are at war with a nationalist movement that has expressed faith in de Gaulle. And de Gaulle, the inherent conservative, works for a liberal Algerian settlement.

Surely before this year ends there must be some definitive settlement. And de Gaulle's curbing of restless army elements is but the start, the preparation for a peace. He cannot afford to relinquish the momentum gained by his recent moves.

The Fifth Republic retains considerable popular backing, while military malcontents lack both leadership and serious public support. They must consequently still submit to the will of the state, now being asserted without equivocation.

The Fourth French Republic ended two years ago with a whimper. But if the Fifth is brought down by another Algerian mob, it will go with a bang.

In 1958 de Gaulle was in the wings, ready to take power. Today he is in power. There is nothing off stage but chaos.

For there seems no longer any choice except between authority in Paris and mob rule from Algiers. Again this nation is torn by multiple schizophrenia. There is the tug between liberalism and reaction, between nineteenth-century dream and twentieth-century reality.

But, whereas two years ago there was an alternative to anarchy in de Gaulle himself, today there is no alternative. There is no second de Gaulle.

As each hour passes there is closer liaison between the proud French army and the revolting settlers of Algeria. De Gaulle always assumed a strong Government could enforce its will on its officers and soldiers. So far he has been proved wrong.

A strange alliance is shaping up. The settlers, most of whom supported Pétain during the last war, feel de Gaulle has no love for them. They resent his promise of Algerian self-determination instead of guaranteed French rule. Their sentiments are understandable but their logic is outdated.

De Gaulle once told me: "There are many discontented people but they do not represent a power. You cannot make France with a Poujade" (the petty fascist). But one can unmake France with a Poujade—if he is supported by the army.

And the street gangs of Algiers are eroding de Gaulle's control over that army. The army's commanders refuse to rout these gangs out of their seditious strongholds.

De Gaulle is as eager as anybody to avoid shedding of the nation's blood. Nevertheless, he clearly sees the need for disciplinary action.

Yet, if he would be resolute and risk violence, his generals are either disobedient—or disobeyed. The French army so far refuses to fight Frenchmen. And its commanders receive the chieftains of the mutineers.

This is an embittered army, overrun in World War II, squeezed out of Syria, Lebanon, Morocco, and Tunisia, defeated in Indochina, deprived of victory in Algeria. It is brave, well trained, and deeply suspicious. It is impregnated by the political techniques of Mao Tse-tung and Tito. Although it remains anti-Communist, one might call it socialist-nationalist.

The danger is that this army, while proclaiming allegiance to the state, may in fact mutiny against state policy. It is already on a sit-down strike, refusing to use force against Frenchmen for the sake of France.

The army may ultimately seize real power in Algeria, while affirming allegiance to de Gaulle, in order to block the rule of civilian hotheads. But this would be a sham: two French states, governed from Algiers and from Paris.

And if the army takes this step, it is hard to see where the giddiness might end. This same army has long toyed with plans to invade Tunisia, where Algeria's Moslem rebels are based. A military junta in Algiers could provoke an African war.

When one regards tranquil Paris it is hard to realize how desperate the situation is. There are none of those ugly salad-basket trucks filled with armed constabulary, which squatted like black beetles while the Fourth Republic died. This capital is calm for the simple reason that few people know what is going on.

Nevertheless, France faces its gravest danger since the German occupation. Right-wing leaders are commencing to wobble in their support of de Gaulle. Fascists once again begin to murmur. And the Communist Politburo calls for a popular front.

This is a fierce, sad contest, following lines long foreordained, like some terrible Greek tragedy. As de Gaulle himself, alone and aging, fights grimly to preserve the unity of France and to restore its grandeur, France itself divides.

De Gaulle rightly perceives: "If I should fail in my task, the unity, prestige, and fate of France would be compromised."

So, one might add, would the unity, prestige, and fate of the Western world.

De Gaulle said in 1956 that only great circumstances produce great men. Pursuing the subject when he was back in power as President of the Fifth Republic, I asked him whether he thought that giants might appear again. He answered:

"When the situation is grave the giants come nearer to a return. Also, you must remember, people grow in stature. People speak of giants when it is all over. Sophocles said that one must wait until the evening to see how splendid the day has been."

It is now evening for France and, as the sun sets, clouds lumber overhead like leaden whales. And it is evening for de Gaulle, a massive, resolute, aging man with weakened eyesight, called for the third time to save his country's unity and honor.

Throughout de Gaulle's life he prepared himself assiduously for the role that lay ahead, that of a chief. "In the face of events," he wrote as a young officer, "it is toward himself that the man of character turns. . . . He stands erect, takes a firm position, and faces these events." In his book *Edge of the Sword,* written thirty years ago, he first described the qualities of a giant.

A leader, he wrote, is aware of risks; and does not "scorn the consequences; but he measures them in good faith and accepts them without evasion. He embraces action with the pride of the master. . . .

"The man of character confers nobility on his acts. . . . Difficulty attracts the man of character, for in grasping difficulty he fulfills himself. . . . Come what may he seeks the bitter joy of responsibility. . . .

"A chief is aloof, for there is no authority without prestige nor prestige without aloofness. Below him, people murmur about his arrogance and his hard demands. But when crisis comes they will follow him, who lifts the burden with his own arms, though they may break, and bears it on his back, though it be broken. . . .

"A feeling of solitude is, according to Faguet, 'the misery of superior men.' . . . One must take sides and the choice is cruel. . . . Before an antique and noble monument someone said to Bonaparte 'It is sad'; and he replied, 'Yes, it is sad, like grandeur.' "

Isolated and ill-served by lesser men with whom he had surrounded his loneliness, de Gaulle misjudged the current paroxysm. He did not give sufficient weight to simmering conspiracies. He could not imagine his frustrated officers would fail to respond to firm commands. He refused to conceive that, under the umbrella of a French Naguib, French Nassers might scheme against the state.

Nevertheless, he has made his "cruel choice." France will react to his vibrant leadership. This is not like Spain's Civil War, when Franco led troops from Morocco into Europe. Dissident forces in Algeria which refuse to fire on seditious Frenchmen there are unlikely to invade France itself, as they planned to do in 1958, to fire on other Frenchmen here.

De Gaulle has waited, as Lincoln waited in an agony, watching the advance of secession and the imminence of war, before he ordered Fort Sumter's relief. But in the end Lincoln moved, accepting responsibility "without evasion."

All week de Gaulle's position has been like that of Asquith, faced at Curragh in 1914 with the mutiny of a British army commanded by generals sympathetic to North Irish insurrectionists. But Asquith was saved by World War I. The mutineers marched on to die in Flanders.

No such desperate external solution presents itself to de Gaulle as he "stands erect, takes a firm position, and faces these events." This is the evening when giants are judged by their own qualities and standards. The challenge is pure and terrible. As the General met it, immutable, implacable, inflamed, one of Europe's greatest statesmen observed: "Yes. He is sometimes insupportable—but he is magnificent."

SIX

The Great Mute Strives to Speak

February 1960

There would have been no such desperate Algerian crisis had France's professional army been truly loyal to the state. The civilian *ultras* alone were helpless and lacking effective strength.

This is not, however, the same as saying that the 200,000 professional officers and noncoms comprising the army's core are perforce disloyal. Rather, by force of circumstance, they have become a body of displaced persons no longer integrated into French society. General Paul Bailly of the Supreme War Council calls this army the "Great Mute."

The army has become a separate organism within the nation's social structure, yet divided from it. It recognizes the need for strong government. It demands a "French Algeria" as, at last, a sign of victory. It wants its unity acknowledged.

De Gaulle, however, is ready, if needed, to shatter this shibboleth of unity to preserve the unity of France. This shibboleth of unity is revered even by the army's noble father confessor, General Ely, who, in 1958, had resigned as Chief of Staff to preserve it while the Fourth Republic fell. The 200,000 professionals instill it in the conscripts who serve with them. They preach their mystical feeling of an organic body, a French party outside France.

For fifteen years these professionals have had scant contact with France. They lived in occupied Germany, in the Orient and Africa, alternating between comfort and arduous excitement, away from the democratic body politic. Like mercenaries, loyal only to their captains, they have shifted between foreign battlefields and foreign barracks.

From 1945 to 1954 the equivalent of three-fifths of the graduating class at St. Cyr, France's West Point, were killed each year in colonial wars and the other two-fifths wounded. Meanwhile France became increasingly noncolonial and antimilitaristic.

The officers lost their favored-class position. There were fewer brilliant marriages to the daughters of the rich. The "prestige of uniform" faded. And, as the army fought to preserve a shrinking empire, it found itself blamed for successive defeats by civilians contented to yield that empire.

Educated in Indochina and frustrated in Algeria, this army conceived savage contempt for the "bourgeois intellectuals" at home. Its "activists" were told by General Chassin, now suspected of complicity in plots: "It is time for the army to cease being deaf and dumb. The time has come to apply certain [Communist] methods."

The "activists" discovered their own elite, the paratroopers. This elite resents the brutish reputation fastened to it by French intellectuals. As veterans of its large corps are released to civilian life, they form a reserve for those who would fish in troubled waters.

Regard the "para" malcontents of the 1958 and 1960 troubles: General Massu; Colonels Marcel Bigeard, Ducasse, Trinquier, Thomazo. Pierre Lagaillarde of the Algiers barricades is a former parachutist; so is Jean-Marie Le Pen, the arrested Right-wing Deputy.

The professional army has become a kind of French Janissary Corps, almost a sect. If any military coup is ever staged in France, it will be made by the captains and the colonels. They might move in the shadow of rank as Nasser moved in General Naguib's shadow. But the dynamists, infected by Communist techniques, yet aspiring to a Rightist "Christian" state, are inflamed by men for the most part little known.

Some day, after the current crisis, de Gaulle must reintegrate this exile army into France's social structure. Otherwise, impelled by different habits of thought, a feeling of apartness and neglect, and resentment born of adversity, it may again seek to remake the fat motherland in its own perplexed image.

"A little rebellion, now and then, is a good thing," Jefferson told Madison, "and as necessary in the political world as storms in the physical." Now that the insurrection of the *ultras* in Algeria has ended one may scrutinize it in that philosophical light.

Jefferson would be proved right if, by this "little rebellion," the political health of France could be improved. But the task is immense; all basic factors that combined to produce the recent crisis still exist. If they cannot be remedied there is bound to be more trouble.

The war between Moslem nationalists and France continues. Both the French army and the French settlers still oppose all thought of peace negotiations and de Gaulle's idea of Algerian self-determination. The professional officer corps must be removed from politics. And de Gaulle's own Government requires a purge of equivocators while fascist-minded plotters are sought out.

All these problems join in the word "Algeria." That unhappy land has become not only a cancer in the body politic but a cause for paranoia in the lucid French brain. Last week, at the height of the troubles, only the satiric weekly *Le Canard Enchaîné* had the courage to face the real issue.

"People of France," it wrote, "you are being made fun of. For five years they have been taking your sons and your money for a war of which you don't approve. For five years they have been telling you tales, lies. In 1958 you said 'yes' to have peace, but you still haven't seen it. One forty-five-millionth of the population is laying down the law for forty-four million Frenchmen. That is enough!"

The settlers still argue that de Gaulle's self-determination policy equals Algeria's eventual independence. They can scarcely be considered wrong. A communiqué published January 19 by the rebels' National Liberation Front says it is "one of the ways of regaining independence."

Likewise, it is difficult to apply de Gaulle's promise that after a cooling-off period he would protect every political opinion in Algeria, prior to a referendum on its future. Would the French army safeguard those favoring Algeria's secession?

Alain Savary, a former Socialist Minister, advocates a ten-year transition of "decolonization" after the fighting ends, with international guarantees to both Moslems and French settlers. But the army, thirsty for victory after a drought of barren wars, is unlikely to accept this. It feels that any step leading to Algeria's independence would make nonsense of still another costly campaign.

Yet, to release France's politically minded army will require much time and greater authority than de Gaulle has hitherto claimed. This is why the General seeks even more legal powers in order to accelerate the momentum he has now gained toward definitive solutions.

Under the Fifth Republic's Constitution de Gaulle could, in fact, proclaim himself tantamount to dictator, a role into which he is now being projected by events. But, despite his highhanded methods, he dislikes the thought of dictatorship and has so far carefully shunned it.

Nevertheless, curious reference was made in an extraordinary speech by de Gaulle to "the national legitimacy which I have embodied for the past twenty years." Like King Louis XVIII, when the Bourbon throne was restored after the First Republic and Bonaparte, de Gaulle seems to annul as nonlegitimate all Governments between the Third and Fifth Republics.

The meaning, if not the text, of the present Constitution is in the process of being changed as de Gaulle consolidates his regime to curb the army, root out remaining centers of conspiracy, and press for Algerian peace. But what will come after he finishes this work, if he succeeds?

Intricate and deeply perplexing problems still face France as, for the second time in two years, it withdraws from the verge of suicide. Even if Algeria can be settled and the army restored to a proper republican role, how can Gaullism be prepared to govern France without de Gaulle? Or would it?

There was vast relief in Washington when de Gaulle put down the extremists in Algeria and moved against conspirators in France. Again the United States realized how much the Western alliance depends upon France, the keystone of NATO's arch, home of its military and political headquarters, and site of its main supply lines.

America's relations with its oldest ally are not easy. If anything, they will become still more difficult as de Gaulle seeks to re-establish France's national pre-eminence. Time and again the General has confirmed his belief that if he adopts an uncompromising attitude the United States in the end will yield. This assumption seems to be proving correct once more in the instance of atomic weapons and, perhaps, NATO commands.

The French mind expects more logic of other nations than of itself. It considers America's parallel effort to sustain both Arab nationalism and the French alliance as, in practice, an absurb contradiction. The fact of the matter is, of course, that diplomacy is the art of the possible, not an exercise in pure reason.

The recent French crisis briefly illuminated the stormy political scene with a brilliant flash of lightning, but in no sense did it sweep away the clouds on the horizon. This storm has yet to blow itself out, and the thunder is coming from the Right.

General de Gaulle, armed with an authority never before granted to a republican chief of state, has begun to rip apart an extensive network of conspiracy that apparently was scheming not merely to force a change in policy but of regime.

Numerous plotters, few of whom are well known abroad, are already in prison. Warrants have been issued for the arrest of others. And a dark tangle of secret societies, some of them linked to the reactionary prewar Cagoulards and some tainted with more recent fascist hues, are under investigation. In addition to tape-recorded conversations monitored by the police, there are some twenty pounds' worth of listed suspects to be interrogated.

The conspiratorial skein was prematurely exposed by General Massu's indiscreet interview. The inspirers of what seems to have been an extensive plot hoped to start their action later. They had not yet completed underground arrangements with sympathizers in the army, arrangements that contemplated action by commanders in both Algeria and Europe.

Now that de Gaulle's police are hot on the trail, many hitherto silent opponents are being forced to declare themselves. What emerges is a picture of Right-wing politicians, ranging from the lunatic fringe of fascism to respected conservatives, apparently linked with disgruntled army officers.

The opposition is being smoked out. Jacques Soustelle has been discharged from the Cabinet and is now openly working against the regime's policy. Georges Bidault, former Premier, has rashly cabled declarations of sympathy to two imprisoned suspects, including Lagaillarde, former leader of the *ultras*.

There are plain hints that these men, together with certain other renowned conservatives, are uniting in feverish efforts to test again the resolution of de Gaulle. The recent rioting at Amiens, aimed against the Government's agricultural program, is symptomatic of other troubles to be expected.

De Gaulle's enemies realize they must move fast. He is now pressing a serious purge of professional army officers. And the opposition knows it will be crippled if deprived of the support of what de Gaulle calls "the accommodating uncertainty of various military elements."

So far only three generals—Jacques Faure (a Poujadiste previously involved in plots), André Gribius, and Henri Mirambeau—have been relieved of their commands. Several others are being investigated. And a packet of colonels has been disciplined.

De Gaulle has also curbed that politically minded militia, the Algerian Home Guard, whose officers had helped to arm rebellious factions. And the army's psychological-warfare division in Algeria, anti-Communist but influenced by the techniques of Mao Tse-tung, has been dissolved.

The advantage of initiative, as well as evident popular support, lies with de Gaulle. The disparate opposition seems to have been caught off balance. But the contest is not over. Before any new dramatic move to end the war against Moslem nationalists in Algeria, there will be further incidents in France.

Washington, now pondering the advisability of giving atomic help to France, would be more generously inclined once the Algerian hurdle has been crossed.

The test of army discipline is probably imminent. If, as appears likely, the Moslem rebels ask a parley, the U.S. should be able swiftly to judge the effectiveness of de Gaulle's control over his restless officers. And once that control is favorably assessed, the way should be opened to granting its ally France some of the assistance it seeks.

NATO will some day have to reckon with the altered situation. There must be agreement among Western nuclear powers on co-ordinating approaches outside Europe—even if this is not in the precise form desired by de Gaulle. Eventually it would be sensible to give the French certain nuclear arms in return for promises to use such weapons as NATO requires. Finally, if the U.S. wants France to continue contributing to alliance defenses at the present level, the easiest way to reduce the French burden for nuclear arms is to make some of its own available—when it is satisfied these will be deployed within the NATO framework.

These matters require delicate diplomacy. In aiding

France the United States cannot risk offending other allies. But there is no doubt this country now qualifies for special treatment. This should be acknowledged as soon as, by meeting the test of Algerian peace, de Gaulle erases political threats from his discontented army. Nobody wishes to confide secrets to a regime that might be ousted by uncertain elements.

Apart from this it is foolish to resent France's entry into the nuclear club, from which there is no blackball. One cannot apply such a blackball after the event.

March 1960

April, T. S. Eliot advises us, is the cruellest month, but for Khrushchev it is likely to be March. The Soviet boss is coming to Paris March 15 in the hope of weaning de Gaulle from his Western ties. He will go home disappointed.

Undoubtedly Khrushchev would like to split the Western front before the summit talks and undoubtedly he has chosen France as the subject for such a splitting operation. This is a mistake. For, if the allies find de Gaulle difficult, Khrushchev will find him adamant.

This will become plain when the word "Berlin" is mentioned. The Russians chose to manufacture an unneeded crisis there in order to provoke big-power talks. They are now applying new presummit pressures. These leave de Gaulle unmoved. He sees no sense in giving Khrushchev what he wants or in being panicked into an unreasonable course.

Thus, on anything important, Khrushchev will learn de Gaulle has nothing to yield to any blandishment. And what kind of blandishments does Khrushchev have to offer?

He cannot promise to cut his links with France's massive Communist party. Or, if he does, nobody will believe him. Anyway, de Gaulle doesn't really care.

He cannot promise to give de Gaulle Soviet nuclear weapons. De Gaulle intends to build his own atomic arsenal. He doesn't even plan to ask the United States to share these deadly stores. Furthermore, Khrushchev can't offer France what he refused to give his ally China.

Nor can he promise to help de Gaulle solve the Algerian war. Khrushchev doesn't control the rebel F.L.N. In fact, F.L.N. Communist sympathizers have recently lost ground.

Thus Khrushchev comes to Paris in burgeoning March with high hopes, a bag full of propaganda, but nothing substantial to trade. And all he should expect to take away with him is happy memories.

We in the West have sometimes grumbled that de Gaulle is an awkward and even embarrassing partner. But Khrushchev will find that he is indeed our partner—and, as a diplomat, perhaps the toughest and most resolute of them all. There will be no deals in Paris between Khrushchev and de Gaulle.

Political traveling is nothing new for Russian bosses; it merely became outmoded under Lenin and Stalin. And the vicissitudes of history have prevented or discouraged official trips like Khrushchev's since Czar Nicholas II came to Paris in 1896. There exist certain vague similarities between the mood of France then and the mood of France today. Twenty-six years before Nicholas's arrival, the French had been smashed in war. Twenty years before Khrushchev's arrival the event was repeated.

When Paris entertained Czar Nicholas, the official account

recalls, "France was questioning herself. But she never despaired. On the morrow of her defeat she courageously applied herself to the task of recovery, rebuilding, revival and restoration which she has since then never ceased." The Czar applauded such efforts. He was stuffed with crayfish soup, trout, lamb, quail, chicken, grouse, and truffled ortolans, and rewarded his hosts by reaffirming an alliance against Germany.

Khrushchev would also like to stimulate in France a parallel German policy. Already the two countries agree that Germany's eastern border should run along the Oder-Neisse Line and (although they don't say so) that a divided Germany is convenient. But de Gaulle has no intention of yielding to Russian demands on Berlin or, for that matter, anything else. Nor is he interested in alliance. Khrushchev may get a bird; he won't get a pact.

May 1960

General de Gaulle's stature has never been higher abroad than it is now, nor has any foreigner visited the United States in recent years who could speak with as much personal prestige. He has successfully re-created a myth of France's grandeur and this, combined with his lofty character, enabled him to approach the President of the greatest Western power as an equal, something no other Frenchman has done in more than two decades. De Gaulle believes these three should speak as equals: Washington for the Americas, London for the Commonwealth, and Paris for the Continent. "We don't exclude the other allies," he says. "But they are less important and this fact must be acknowledged."

De Gaulle has been as consistent in demanding a greater French role in the Western alliance as he has been on Algerian self-determination. He wants some commitment that America will consult France as well as Britain on major world issues. And, although the United States came to the brink of such a commitment during the summit crisis, it has eschewed giving it.

All that is now needed is some assurance—either in a public statement or in a private letter from Eisenhower to de Gaulle—that the Western Big Three chiefs of government will meet when needed and that their foreign ministers will consult more frequently. This would only recognize a situation that, in fact, already exists. De Gaulle has seen Eisenhower twice this year and the Big Three foreign ministers manage to keep up what is almost an international commuters' bridge game.

Yet de Gaulle's position in France itself is paradoxically less secure. Had the revolt against his authority not exploded prematurely last January, this country might now be in the throes of crisis and the Gaullist regime endangered. For there is considerable evidence that the network of conspiracies uncovered since the last Algiers uprising planned to move against de Gaulle at this precise instant, while he was in the United States. Only the indiscretions of General Massu, a loyal but foolish man, and the stupidity of certain nervous key conspirators, exposed the plot three months early and enabled de Gaulle to squash it.

As a result the anti-Gaullist elements are disorganized and off balance; but they still exist.

The courteous, quiet shake-up has involved many generals, some of whom were due to retire anyway, some of whom were scheduled for promotion, and some of whom were shifted from the turbulent Algerian scene. The professional officer corps is scarcely happy. A widespread purge of army generals has restored military discipline. Nevertheless, the disgruntlement of numerous officers frustrated by the Algerian war remains. Various underground movements, almost all of them linked in one or another way to the *ultras* of Algiers, continue to scheme, to publish inflammatory declarations, and to work for de Gaulle's overthrow. So far, however, these disparate secret committees appear to lack centralized direction.

De Gaulle told Eisenhower at Camp David that his Algerian program remained unchanged from his September 1959 promise of self-determination. Eisenhower expressed full support and even suggested this be mentioned in the communiqué reviewing their talks. But de Gaulle, regarding Algeria as an internal matter, thought such mention inadvisable.

Instead he promised to refer to Algeria in his New York speech on April 26. There he said: "As for Algeria . . . we want the destiny of this country to be decided by the Algerians and only by the Algerians." Eisenhower commented afterward: "On that basis, just as I did in September, 1959, I endorsed what you were doing and wish you well in its progress."

The United States is now firmly behind the Gaullist formula for Algerian peace. On his part, de Gaulle ended all doubts about his intentions by reiterating them a few days ago with sufficient precision to incur the wrath of France's Right-wing politicians. Armistice talks may start very soon.

June 1960

After six weeks of turbulence and reviving cold war one may take comfort that there is at last a real prospect of settling the conflict between France and the Algerian National Liberation Front. Excepting the artillery duel off China's coast, that conflict is the world's only hot war. And if it can be ended there is a chance of vastly improving the Western position in Europe, Africa, and the Middle East.

In no sense can one assume that merely because de Gaulle and the F.L.N. have agreed to start talking peace they will succeed in making peace. Negotiations are bound to be complex and long. F.L.N. extremists will have many opportunities to upset the parleys by recourse to violence. And French extremists will undoubtedly try to muster army support to frustrate Gaullist policy.

Nevertheless, with persistence of purpose and subtlety of maneuver, de Gaulle has produced a situation which for the first time makes settlement possible. His comments about an "Algerian Algeria" and "association" with France are sufficiently vague to allow much room for bargaining.

De Gaulle has attained such immense renown that there can be little doubt a heavy majority of Frenchmen will accept almost any Algerian solution he endorses. His opponents, led by some highly intelligent and prestigious politicians, have been at a disadvantage ever since last January's attempted Algiers *Putsch*. The people of France if not the politicians of France are with their President.

July 1960

France's most serious long-range problem is how to keep Gaullism after de Gaulle has gone, or, in other words, how to insure a peaceful return to normal government. For the Fifth Republic, with its dynamism, its flair for grandeur, and its one-man administration, is not normal. With "Mongénéral," observes a Paris satirical weekly, the French people "have gotten over genius."

De Gaulle is now sixty-nine years old. His is a family blessed with longevity. In a Mendelian sense, he should be fit to govern France for another decade. Nevertheless, politics and genetics are separate fields. There is acute, if rarely spoken, interest in what form of government France shall have when General de Gaulle no longer reigns and whether any preparations are being made for a successor. The same satirical weekly comments: "No doubt the idea of having a successor offends his modesty."

The French fear that, if de Gaulle should suddenly die, no adequate system has been provided in advance to insure that his ideas will be carried out. There can, in fact, be no Gaullism without de Gaulle. This leaves the possibility that, if no proper machinery is arranged in time, he might be succeeded by chaos.

Early this year the problem was put up to the General by a distinguished liberal Gaullist and former Cabinet Minister. De Gaulle seemed surprised and admitted that none of his close associates had previously dared discuss the matter. He asked for a memorandum on the former Minister's ideas. Such a memorandum was submitted this spring and, when he is less preoccupied with immediately critical things, the General promises to pursue the subject.

The memorandum, which comprised twenty pages, complained that the Fifth Republic suffered from two glaring weaknesses. It described these as one-man government, in which de Gaulle is surrounded by Ministers who lack real influence or national prestige; and as the lack of any orderly system of succession.

From this argument the memorandum concluded it was necessary to install in France a system of executive democracy, controlled by checks and balances, similar to that in the United States. It urged a start in this direction as soon as possible, but admitted that, first of all, a means must be found to establish true order by ending the Algerian war (now being attempted) and more intensive social reforms must be instituted to narrow the gap between wealth and poverty. It suggested as a basis for eventual Algerian peace a new kind of Austro-Hungarian monarchy, with the President of France also serving as chief executive of a separate Algerian state.

The memorandum proposed that de Gaulle take the following steps: (1) Appoint a Cabinet of more distinguished French political leaders to give an appearance of less individually concentrated authority; (2) name a commission to define future relationships between Algeria and France and to outline needed social reforms; (3) designate a group to draft a new constitution for the post-Gaullist period; (4) dissolve the National Assembly and call a referendum to approve the new constitution.

The problems posed have not been sufficiently discussed in France; nor have they been sufficiently reviewed by de Gaulle, engrossed as he is in urgently important tasks such as settling the Algerian war. One may indeed hope, as do a majority of French citizens (if not a majority of French politicians), that the General's heritage of longevity will express itself and that he will have many more years in which to stabilize the situation. This would allow preparation for satisfactory ways of passing on the stability achieved. But this is only a hope. The sensible thing would be to start the task right now.

December 1960

All but one of the familiar smells are back in autumnal Paris. There is the fragrance of dead leaves, of dank seaweed in the oyster stalls, and of sweet nougat and sugared nuts in the booths of itinerant venders. And there is that oddly agreeable odor of mist and coal smoke. The only missing smell is the smell of danger.

Now this is curious because, normally, when there is danger in the air of Paris you can almost sniff it. All through those months of 1958 while the Fourth Republic was dying, one could detect its developing corruption. And last December and early January, before the *Putsch* exploded in Algiers, sensitive nostrils knew that trouble imminently lurked.

Such is not the case today. There is no strange, prethunderous calm or scent of coming crisis. There is merely an atmosphere of tranquillity. Yet this is a deceptive atmosphere because again there is danger in the air.

The principal threat comes from conservative elements. Fifteen known conspiratorial organizations hope either to frustrate de Gaulle's Algerian policy or to overthrow his Government. And if fifteen such groups are careless enough to let themselves be known, one wonders how many others exist.

No faction either in France or in Algeria is strong enough to move effectively unless it has military backing. And de Gaulle has disciplined his army. Nevertheless, seventeen generals so violently disagree with him on Algeria that their ultimate intentions are, to say the least, uncertain.

Some of them have retired from active military duty and some have not. But none of them has retired from politicking. And their opinions filter down to captains and lieutenants charged with protecting Moslem Algerian villagers against Moslem Algerian rebels and sometimes wondering why they fight.

De Gaulle is acutely aware of the diehard opposition. He has moved most of his troops out of Algiers, grand capital of Balkan plots, and replaced them with tough gendarmes. He has shifted and reshifted commanders and officials, only to watch their replacements infected by new doubts.

The time of cauterization has come. Just as the U.N. begins once more to debate the feverish Algerian question, the General prepares to visit the scene of trouble and, with the magnetism of his personality, to rally his officers behind him. Soon thereafter he will test the climate of opinion in France itself by posing the issue of his policy in a national referendum. Then, it is clear, he will take decisive steps.

De Gaulle has trump cards still to play. Many new African states support him; and Tunisia—which shelters the rebels—nevertheless argues that de Gaulle is the best single hope for peace. However, at the extremes, the climate has changed. Since the breakdown of summit talks, Russia has begun to support the Algerian insurrectionists, and Communist sympathizers are gaining influence among them. It is not in Moscow's interest to see an end to a war that weakens France and drains NATO.

Likewise, European settlers in Algeria fear peace by compromise. De Gaulle's mention of an "Algerian Republic" has brought them to the verge of desperation. They hope to persuade their army friends to stage a sit-down strike if those same European settlers once again mount the barricades. There is chaos in the offing even if the scent of danger today is absent from the pleasant air of France.

One week ago I wrote that there was "danger in the air" of France but it had not yet begun to produce its familiar smell. Three days later Lagaillarde, the poor man's D'Artagnan, and other anti-de Gaulle conspirators had skipped to Spain. The familiar smell is back.

So far this scent of danger is only faintly perceptible, like that of homogenized pot-cheese. It has by no means achieved the rich odor of ripe Camembert that usually accompanies French crisis, as in 1958 or last winter. But the chances are it may—and soon.

There are relatively minor riots in Algeria. Already just a few more gendarmes have begun to appear around key Paris administrative centers. Here and there one sees police "salad baskets."

Some of the seventeen generals known to sympathize with plotters are issuing unsolicited loyalty professions. General Salan, who carries more rank than prestige, waits in Spain, where *ultra* agents confer with Franco's brother-in-law, the unsavory Serrano Suner.

Three politicians anxious to repace de Gaulle have found reasons for going abroad. Conspiratorial networks are muttering to each other across Interior Ministry wire taps and monitored secret radio channels.

On both extremes, Algerian rebel and French, assassins

keep their weapons oiled—from the officially paid if officially disavowed Red Hand to the F.L.N.'s own "Murder Incorporated." The former specializes in knocking off rebel agents and European munitions merchants who supply them. The latter levies tribute and directs lead at opponents in France.

This week I invited to lunch a friend who bears six recent bullet holes. He declined all thought of eating in a public restaurant. Instead he chatted dolefully in my house while his armed bodyguard sat outside keeping uneasy watch.

Next month's referendum will show that at least 70 per cent of metropolitan Frenchmen support de Gaulle's program to end the war. We will soon see whether the dead-end, *ultra* bitter boys can explode another bomb to frustrate progress.

If France's army wavers in its loyalty, a terrible storm brews. The odds, I must emphasize, remain in favor of settlement, thanks to de Gaulle's determination and prestigious personality. Yet there are clouds on the horizon; and from Algeria a south wind blows.

Still more splendor has, if anything, been added to de Gaulle's splendid character by the brutal Algerian events. Nevertheless, as far as political reality is concerned, his stormy voyage did nothing save shatter illusions.

The first illusion, fostered by those who would like to keep Algeria a part of France, was that the Moslem majority shared this wish. That dream vanished in the blood-spattered casbahs of Algiers and Oran. The second illusion, encouraged by extremists on both Mediterranean shores, was that the army would turn against de Gaulle. This did not occur.

The General himself believes "Those who govern the country and those who direct its armed forces are, to some extent, estranged from one another." But he proved that when a Chief of State displays iron will and courage, even a disgruntled army will obey him.

Illusions, indeed, were smashed. And now we see naked emotions, religious bias, and racial savagery, exposed in all their ugliness. "Things are in the saddle," as Emerson once said, "and ride mankind."

Nobody can foretell where these "things" will lead. Undoubtedly the most terrible direction would be the road to Algerian partition. For, were this to come about, it would not only formalize the grim war between France and Moslem nationalists; it would insure the persistence of hatred for many decades.

However, there is grave danger that, *de facto,* such a partition could impose itself; that *ultras* might suddenly seize the fertile shore and rich cities from Algiers to Oran and create the equivalent of a French "Israel," surrounded by Arab nationalists.

De Gaulle himself occasionally hinted at partition in an effort to force truce negotiations. But his true dream envisions a fully free Algeria, a harmonious community of many races and religions, bound to France in co-independence. This dream is dying. As de Gaulle himself would say: "The spectacle of a sick man shaking his fist at death can leave no one unmoved."

The brave old President is a disciple of the philosopher Henri Bergson. Bergson taught that the only way the human mind can directly contact reality is by intuition, by combining instinct with intelligence; that instinct alone can give the concrete feel of knowledge.

Therefore, despite doubts among his ministers, de Gaulle pressed his intuitive feeling that Algeria could be freed and simultaneously tied to France. Likewise, despite the advice of his most intimate counselors, he insisted on making his tragically explosive Algerian journey.

De Gaulle's historical role is cruelly paradoxical. Twenty years ago he revolted against a doomed, dispirited Administration and fought to restore France's grandeur and its empire. He succeeded against impossible odds.

Now, one generation later, he tries again—and again against impossible odds—this time to give up peacefully the empire he restored. France has handed liberty to vast provinces of Africa and to reaches of the Indian Ocean from Madagascar to Pondicherry. Yet in Algeria, where reasonably the process should end most satisfactorily in warm bonds between motherland and nearest child, disaster overwhelms cold sense.

De Gaulle is at his best, his noblest, and his most relentless when other men might despond. He has said: "The man of character finds an especial attractiveness in difficulty, since it is only by coming to grips with difficulty that he can realize his potentialities." He is a fighter and a gambler.

From 1958, when he was projected back to power, de Gaulle has never departed from his vision of a sane Algerian solution which would set at rest that sad and bloody land. Occasionally he may have seemed to waver on his course. But this was ruse; for among his qualities is craftiness.

It would be an error, therefore, to think he has departed from his steadfast aim. But events, those Emersonian "things," have begun to run against him. To quote one of his favorite aphorisms: "The smell of the world has changed."

January 1961

President de Gaulle, as always lonely, austere, obstinate, and brave, begins what could be his last battle with the opening of a referendum on his Algerian policy. By Sunday evening Frenchmen and Algerians on both sides of the Mediterranean will have expressed their opinion: approval, disapproval, or indifferent abstention.

There is little doubt that de Gaulle will get a majority in metropolitan France despite the fact that parties claiming more than half the registered electorate urge their membership to vote No. The General commands a massive personal following. And the implied threat that he might resign if his backing is too weak terrifies the average Frenchman. De Gaulle once disrupted France in order to unify it. Now he seeks to unify and avoid disruption. Were he to go, all the inherently conflicting forces seething below the surface would emerge to fight for power. Already they are girding for that possibility.

Pierre Poujade, the petty fascist, has been consulting in Spain with General Salan. Soustelle, the keenly intelligent former Gaullist who broke with the General, meets often with Antoine Pinay. Pinay aspires to succeed de Gaulle as President and Soustelle would be either Premier or Foreign Minister in such a government.

Activists financed by wealthy *ultras* in Algeria have been spreading anti-Gaullist propaganda. And some army chiefs, both retired and active, recognizing that this is the time of decision, are risking pensions or careers in endeavors to encourage opposition.

On the whole, Frenchmen regard the curious artifice of referendum with favor; they like to be consulted. This fact, coupled with war weariness and de Gaulle's magnetism, should induce the majority to support his plan to give Algeria self-determination.

But the vote in Algeria itself is unlikely to demonstrate much. The European minority will oppose de Gaulle. Moslems will be torn between mixed threats and blandishments from both the F.L.N. rebels and France's confused soldiery.

For almost three years de Gaulle has been preparing for this grave event. He has restored stability, leadership, and confidence to his country and has instilled considerable discipline in the army. Obscuring his aims in cryptic if beautifully phrased utterances, he has sought to build national unity by alternately placating Right and Left.

What he hopes to achieve, if backed by enough voters, is the basis for negotiation with the various elements of Algeria, including the F.L.N. His essential idea is to give the Algerians eventual independence, including control of their own foreign policy and a U.N. seat—but with the proviso that rights of Europeans are guaranteed and that defense, economy, and finance remain linked with those of France.

If Algeria opts for complete secession with no guarantees, perforce a *de facto* partition will come about. Europeans would carve out a "French Israel" along the seacoast from Algiers to Oran and thus perpetuate the war.

Should de Gaulle receive what he considers insufficient backing, and retire, the resulting confusion could end in civil war. An army-backed Pinay Government would face an inevitable ruckus with a Left-wing popular front.

The French Right can boast the reputation of being the stupidest Right in the world. Even choice members of the

American Right, men like Senator Barry Goldwater or Senator James Eastland, look like leaders of the *Jacquerie* when compared with the Right of France.

The lunk-headedness of the French Right helped produce a popular front in the nineteen-thirties and eroded the vigor of the Third Republic. The French Right shirked its responsibility of harnessing industry to production of adequate defenses before World War II. Its leaders in the military establishment failed to see that methods of war had changed and, after their defeat, promptly attached themselves to Hitler.

The French Right has never liked General de Gaulle, who disrupted its plans in 1940 by rallying popular support for resistance and eventual victory. The French Right refuses to admit that this is a changing world and aspires to return to the long-lost era of the Bourbons. Like Spain's Tories, it regards with equal distaste Communists, Socialists, labor unions, and Liberals.

Ever since this country's 1789 Revolution, the French Right has managed to attract support from approximately one-third of France's population—a changing group of intrenched inheritors, industrialists, farmers, peasants, and small businessmen. Generation after generation, this conservative third has struggled to assert itself against the other two-thirds of extreme Left and Liberals.

The French Right traditionally seeks to substitute reactionary emotions for the lucid reason which France admires and rarely practices politically. Now, pursuing archaic goals by archaic methods, the French Right is making perhaps its last great stand on the issue of Algeria.

As is so often the sad case in France, the Right has joined with the extreme Left in opposing history's logic. The Communists order followers to vote No in today's referendum on de Gaulle's policy.

To be sure, there are ardent opponents of de Gaulle who are neither Communists nor members of the true Right—men like Bourgès-Maunoury and Soustelle, embittered by events. But the real thunder of opposition that is not led by Moscow is the thunder of the Right.

What would happen if the French Right took power? For a time, backed by the army and spoken for by disgruntled politicians, it might check progress. But it could not check this long. Two-thirds of the people of France would not accept the check. France cannot be remade in the image of the past.

There would be inevitable formation of a popular-front movement, led by Communists. France would split. The democracy so tenuously preserved by de Gaulle's benevolent despotism would dissolve in chaos. And, because the French Right remains in a minority, its experiment would fail.

The French Right seeks its own destruction with the desperate illogic of those lemmings which seasonally drown themselves. Unlike the German, Italian, and British Right, the French Right refuses to adjust to time. It never learns, never forgets, and prefers suicide to coexistence.

Fortunately, one may hope with considerable optimism that because of the towering personal stature of de Gaulle, a liberal much detested by the French Right, and the good sense of independent-minded Frenchmen who ignore party instructions, the referendum will go heavily against the French Right—and against their Communist cobelligerents.

March 1961

The imminence of Algerian peace talks has produced certain changes of attitude in Cairo, which aspires to paramount leadership among the Arab capitals. These changes might be listed accordingly: growing respect for General de Gaulle; realization that President Bourguiba, for long discounted and assailed, is a man to be reckoned with; and an initial feeling of satisfaction that the cause of North African nationalism again seems about to triumph.

But, should parleys between the French and Algeria's rebel chiefs end in accord, there does not yet seem to be full awareness of what the implications for Cairo may ultimately be. If a confederation, however loose, finally evolves among Tunisia, Morocco, and an independent Algeria, we could see an important shift in Arab political relationships.

Hitherto Cairo, sparked by President Nasser's personal magnetism, has sought to assert itself as unrivaled champion of Arabism between the Atlantic and the Persian Gulf. This pretension has by no means wholly been acknowledged. Neither Iraq nor Jordan accepts Nasser's ascendancy. Lebanon maintains an uneasy equilibrium. Saudi Arabian policy shifts but doesn't succumb. And peripheral British-protected sheikhdoms still elude Cairo pressures.

In a way Nasser may be said to have had more success among Arabs to the West. His prestige in Libya is immense. His relations with the Algerians are more than cordial, and he has made signal efforts to gain Moroccan sympathy. To some degree his endorsement of extreme African nationalism is designed to cement these bonds with North African Arabs.

Nevertheless, if an Algerian settlement is arranged, there is likelihood that Nasser's position in these westward regions will diminish and that of pro-French leaders, symbolized by Bourguiba, will grow. Egypt, or what is called the United Arab Republic's southern province, may find itself gradually walled off by a vague commonwealth strongly attracted to the culture and economy of France. And France, even before the Suez war, was regarded as an enemy. Nasser still criticizes the new African states which look on Paris as a friend.

Thus, although Algerian freedom is an avowed goal of U.A.R. policy, it could in the end redound against U.A.R. influence. Should Bourguiba and pro-Western leaders in Algeria gain ascendancy in the *Maghreb,* or northwest African area, the present uneasy Arab power balance will be tipped.

De Gaulle recognizes this. It so happens he does not envision the likelihood of any close confederation among Tunisians, Moroccans, and Algerians. He foresees each nation following its separate destiny in the long run and achieving little more unity than the Middle Eastern Arabs Nasser dreamed of tying together. Nor does he regard this as a matter of primordial importance. In all events he hopes logic will dictate close ties with Paris, similar to those between London and the Commonwealth. Even before he regained authority he foresaw the need for shedding the last vestiges of French colonialism and for creating a Gallic version of Britain's Commonwealth, bound by common ties of language and economy, together reflected in the diplomatic mirror.

The General is determined to end the Algerian war. He has shown as much by attaching no preconditions to the forthcoming talks. He is confident that if Algerian self-determination produces complete independence, as it almost certainly will, a new regime will find it must lean heavily on France for help and guidance. This may well obviate any need for precise legal guarantees for the European minority.

April 1961

President Kennedy's decision to visit General de Gaulle is entirely admirable. The two men, separated in years by more than a generation, are nevertheless today's outstanding Western leaders. They share a belief in the value of strong personal leadership.

When Kennedy arrives he will already have conferred in the United States with Macmillan and Adenauer. But he cannot hope to understand the problems of co-ordinating policy during this epoch of decolonization until he has exchanged views with de Gaulle. When he has done this it is likely his admiration for the General will have been increased. But the President will also discover certain differences between Washington and Paris that cannot, for the time, be reconciled.

In any broad philosophical conversation Kennedy will find de Gaulle convinced that in our era democracies require greater, not less, guidance by their chiefs. While he liked President Eisenhower, de Gaulle did not feel that Kennedy's predecessor exerted sufficient political direction. On this point, no matter how politely it is implied, there will be no dissent with his distinguished guest.

De Gaulle has not yet had occasion to size up the new President. Notwithstanding, he feels the temper of this historical moment will increasingly push Kennedy's Administration toward an ever stronger central executive and that the American economy will find itself increasingly pushed toward what the French call *dirigisme,* or state direction. Should Kennedy inquire further on this point he may hear his host's opinion that the United States will simply have to abandon some of its free-enterprise shibboleths and accept greater controls because the pressures of our age disallow the luxury of *laissez faire.*

Diplomatically speaking, the most fundamental agreement between de Gaulle and Kennedy lies in their essentially similar views on the Common Market and a strong Europe. De Gaulle is a nationalist in the sense of wishing to rebuild a powerful France. He is an anticolonialist in the sense of wishing to end the last vestiges of French empire and make peace in Algeria. And he is an internationalist in the sense of favoring the Common Market.

However, when the two statesmen talk about the U.N. and NATO there will be little accord. Washington is disposed to build up the U.N. and elaborate many of its diplomatic problems through the world organization. De Gaulle, on the other hand, doesn't even admit that the U.N. "exists." He considers it "an augmented Babel" dominated increasingly by irresponsible small African and Asian states subject to Communist suasion. He thinks U.N. intervention in the Congo is ridiculous. While France didn't use its veto power to prevent this operation, it is trying to block its continuation by a financial boycott.

This wholly opposite view on the U.N. is part of a basic chasm between French and American foreign policy. De Gaulle feels the free world needs "a Western policy" but that Washington's policy is not "Western." He considers it as much pro-Nkrumah and pro-Nasser as it is pro-de Gaulle.

De Gaulle sought to encourage formulation of his concept of "Western" policy, but neither Washington nor London endorses his proposal for a Big Three political directorate. He first suggested this in September 1958, in letters to Eisenhower and Macmillan, but the State Department pigeonholed the scheme. It hasn't since been revived. Nor does de Gaulle, a proud man, intend to raise the matter formally again unless Kennedy first broaches it.

It would be wise for Kennedy to do so. For, whether openly recognized or not, this question lies at the heart of all America's difficulties with France in the Afro-Asian world, in the U.N., in NATO, and, ultimately, with China.

Washington and London thought they could resolve the question of the directorate by naming a relatively high-level committee of undersecretaries of foreign affairs to consult with intermittent frequency. But this doesn't satisfy de Gaulle. He wants some kind of commitment to discuss all Western problems regularly and on a global, not merely North Atlantic, scale.

The U.S. has more or less shoved this matter under the rug, but de Gaulle hasn't forgotten it.

Another fundamental problem, sharing nuclear secrets, has never been put forth openly by de Gaulle. But it is a serious diplomatic obstacle. De Gaulle is determined to make France a military nuclear power. He is convinced no nation can be in the first rank without its own atomic arsenal. Therefore, uninvited to join in the Geneva test-ban parleys, he unilaterally builds and tests his own weapons. He will continue to do so until formally admitted to the so-called "nuclear club" or given access to the same kind of help the U.S. provides to the English.

Feeling excluded from the diplomatic intimacy prevailing between Washington and London and feeling excluded from the Anglo-American nuclear partnership, de Gaulle sits on his hands in NATO. De Gaulle refuses to integrate his forces under General Lauris Norstad or to store American atomic warheads. He has eased out U.S. fighter-bomber units, has withdrawn his Mediterranean fleet from allied command, and is now vetoing appointment of a Secretary-General.

Finally, de Gaulle vigorously opposes the idea propounded by Norstad and the Eisenhower Administration of giving NATO its own nuclear stockpile. For him this means simply that the United States, under an apparently novel formula, would in fact continue to control these weapons. Kennedy's recent change in approach doesn't alter the General's attitude.

Kennedy may be surprised, however, to find how "anticolonialist" the General is even though he places scant value on the U.N. By the time they meet, one hopes headway will have been made toward an Algerian settlement. But, regardless, de Gaulle will surely tell his guest that France "has completely abandoned colonialism in all and every form; colonialism is finished."

The difference comes on approaches. France relies more on its vague Community ties with former African colonies than on the U.N. France also wishes to preserve certain strong points such as leased bases at Bizerte and Mers-el-Kebir. And France is very sensitive about the possibility of U.S. power moving its influence into areas of Africa vacated by French power. This very factor contributes to obviously discordant Franco-American views on Southeast Asia. It will therefore be up to President Kennedy to reassure his French peer on this delicate point.

The secret societies, including remnants of prewar *Cagoulards,* wartime fascists, anti-Gaullist zealots, frustrated officers, and Algerian settlers, reorganized some weeks ago in a new Secret Army Organization or O.A.S. This body, working through agents in Geneva, Madrid, and Germany, brought together dissatisfied officers.

At first there seemed little imminent likelihood of open warfare. De Gaulle appears intent on quarantining and starving out the mutineers, and they hope to topple the Government from afar. But, as in previous conspiracies, the rebels had a desperate contingency plan.

This presumably aspires to establish an armed stronghold in the southwest, around the airborne garrison towns of Pau and Toulouse; persuade disaffected French commanders in Germany to back the revolt; and then, simultaneously, land troops in Paris, hoping they wouldn't be opposed.

The personality of France is riven. Imagine a quarrel between the American Government, backed by an overwhelming popular majority, and the entire Marine Corps, aided by army units, based in Puerto Rico, encouraged by the John Birch Society and sponsored by famous retired five-star generals. In terms of logic, such is the situation here.

De Gaulle, unfortunately, misjudged his officers.

This army—meaning the professional cadres—may not wish to be the state; but it clearly wishes to reform or overthrow it. As de Gaulle told me, another time: "Regimes never reform themselves. They simply fall. They collapse." This one will not collapse without a fight.

De Gaulle has a strong Government. Yet, this uprising's

leaders are more talented and significant than the roughnecks or jackanapes like Massu and Faure who preceded them.

Their dangerous gamble cannot possibly end in compromise. The French people are heavily behind de Gaulle; and de Gaulle, a man of resolute courage, does not by nature yield in crises. This crisis, now terrible, is getting swiftly worse.

Philosophically speaking, Charles de Gaulle proved again this week that man can dominate events. By the nobility and resolution of his personal actions he showed the essential folly of such Marxist claptrap as "economic determinism" and "dialectical materialism," doctrines that purport to prove that there are political forces superior to human will.

De Gaulle and de Gaulle alone shattered the latest attempt on his authority. The fact that he was aided by loyal lieutenants and a substantially loyal nation does not alter this conclusion. It was de Gaulle who chose and tempered his lieutenants, who imbued them with resolve even when some of them began to waver, and who served as the symbol around which France could rally. If some of his judgments helped produce the trouble, his powerful character crushed it.

More than any man, at least in modern history, de Gaulle deliberately formed himself to be a man of crisis. In this respect he has been aided by a broad but critically selective study of French sages. From Henri Bergson, the modern philosopher, he learned to trust intuition, to combine instinct with intelligence.

From Philippe Villiers de L'Isle-Adam, a nineteenth-century poet, he learned "to carry glory in one's inmost self."

And from Emile Faguet he learned of the "wretchedness of superior beings," or, as it were, the need for great leaders to accept sad but chosen loneliness from their fellows.

For at least thirty years de Gaulle has intensely studied the technique of leadership and disciplined himself for the task. He recognized the personal sacrifices that must be made to accomplish this aim, the necessity of remaining apart from and above other men to strengthen the "imprint of his personality." To appreciate the self-assurance with which de Gaulle has brushed aside the doubts of those he consulted, one must recognize the moral toughness, the artistic mastery, and the sublime confidence in his own command that rules him.

Oddly enough, the very day before mutinous generals touched off their foolhardy insurrection, which failed so swiftly because of de Gaulle's magnetic personality and Bergsonian intuition, he was writing a letter to a friend "on the never-exhausted theme of the encounter of man with death."

But one does not need the reflection of posterity to measure de Gaulle. To use his own Sophoclean terms, this day is perceptibly splendid while the sun still shines. De Gaulle has set himself as a task the restoration to France of its lost "grandeur." On the scale of which he dreams that would appear insuperable. But the grandeur of his own personality is nevertheless mirrored in the French people, above all in their moments of trial. He is injecting a new dignity into a nation accustomed to dignity.

Those who do not know de Gaulle may cavil at many of his policies and at his approach to democracy, which is that of a benevolent despot but which has the intention of a benevolent custodian. Yet they may be thankful he is in the seat of power. By some strange prescience, he prepared himself for this lonely, resolute role which is determined to lead to peace in unhappy Algeria.

When General de Gaulle was projected back to power he saw he must accomplish three things before order could be restored to France and peace to its blood-soaked Algerian appanage.

He had to shrink Communist strength. To a degree he succeeded in doing this although, deprived of open constitutional vigor, the party remains firmly organized. He had to fragment the extreme political Right, which he has largely achieved. And he had to purge the army of activists and reassert the discipline of civilian authority.

Here the General sadly failed. The hard-bitten professional officer corps, at no time particularly Gaullist, disgruntled by twenty-one years of unsuccessful fighting, has again risen. Although Algeria has been the perpetual battlefield, the struggle is between France and its own army.

This is the gravest crisis since that which murdered the Fourth Republic.

Two things are clear. Algerian peace prospects have been retarded, perhaps indefinitely. And France's political structure, no matter who wins this grim contest, must change. The mutinous generals and colonels know they can expect no quarter. Paris will see some form of dictatorship before this ghastly quarrel ends—as implied by de Gaulle's emergency measures before the April assault loomed.

Appearances in the lovely illuminated capital are deceptive. There was utter calm but now special police dispositions are forming in the city. Those few suspects arrested were picked up with discretion. Even the multiplication of horrid plastic-bomb explosions still seems trivial. But tanks and trucks of armed *gendarmerie* are rolling in the outskirts.

Nevertheless, this conspiracy is more cleverly and efficiently planned than its predecessors. It was originally timed for April 24. However, when the Government sniffed trouble, Colonel Yves Godard, a veteran of other plots, triggered this one prematurely.

May 1961

One aftermath of the recent crisis is a deliberate effort to poison Franco-American relationships. Not surprisingly, one may trace the origins of this propaganda campaign to Moscow. But, unfortunately, it has been abetted by rumor-mongering of certain anti-American French officials. Furthermore, the waters have unconsciously been troubled by enthusiastic but naïve persons in Washington.

To set the record straight—the U.S. Government behaved with discretion, wisdom, and propriety during the insurrection. This applies to all branches—the embassy (and consulate general in Algiers), the C.I.A., and American armed forces. Ambassador James Gavin transmitted a message from President Kennedy to the Elysée Palace on the night of April 22. He did not ask to see the overburdened de Gaulle, but discreetly handed Mr. Kennedy's letter to his principal aide, adding a few sympathetic words.

The letter offered support and any help requested but ventured no tactless suggestions of armed assistance that might have offended the proud French Chief of State. On April 27 Gavin saw de Gaulle and, after presenting another Kennedy letter congratulating the General, briefly discussed other matters.

No American in Algeria had to do with any insurrectional leader. General Charles C. Smith, Jr., Paris Military Attaché, was in Algiers on a routine trip. He withdrew to the Sahara. No consular employee saw any rebel. The only contact was indirect, through the Swiss dean of the corps, who demanded diplomatic transmission facilities.

Nor did any agents of the Central Intelligence Agency see sympathizers with the junta. Like the French Government, the C.I.A. knew another plot was brewing to prevent Algerian peace negotiations. But, like French security services, it knew nothing of the timing. The C.I.A. co-operated with the French—when they solicited this. Apart from that it stuck to its task of informing Washington.

United States commanders were alerted that "unauthorized" elements might seek to seize American installations. They were ordered to block such endeavors by all means short of armed action. Landing fields would have been covered with obstacles in case the Algerian junta sought to land airborne units. But our troops were told to lay low and keep silent.

Unfortunately, enthusiasts in Washington apparently exaggerated these friendly and correct acts and made our gestures of support seem like unsolicited offers of military aid. De Gaulle didn't want this and presumably resents the implication. Mr. Kennedy volunteered all help requested. None was.

Nevertheless, our name is now being sullied in the French press and by inspired rumors. Even the reputable *Le Monde* wrote: "It appears well established that American agents more or less encouraged Maurice Challe" (the junta leader). Less-respected journals printed even more wicked stories. These hint that since Washington disagreed with de Gaulle on NATO, the C.I.A. wanted him overthrown.

When one checks, one finds all this began in a Moscow *Izvestia* article April 25. It was embellished and spread around Paris by the Polish Press Attaché. When the Russian Ambassador tried the tale on a group of high French officials, one of them inquired cynically: "Excellency, do you think the C.I.A. also had agents with Marshal Zhukov?"

Since the Cuban disaster the C.I.A. has unfortunately been on the spot. Too many people are tempted to believe silly things about it. Thus the ground for hostile propaganda was prepared. And it was easy to fabricate fables of evil purpose because it was known Challe favored integration of French forces in NATO and de Gaulle doesn't.

But the United States plays no policy of *Putsch* against its allies. It may argue differences but it respects partners. And it would be lunacy to imagine, with its evident desire to further decolonialization, that the U.S. would hope to oust the one Frenchman resolved and able to make peace in Algeria on the basis of self-determination.

There is no point dignifying malice by official protest. It will evaporate in illogic. But let us also hope well-intended American propagandists will cease claiming, even by innuendo, that the U.S. played any significant role in quelling the *coup d'état*. The victory was de Gaulle's.

The mere fact that France begins formal negotiations with the rebel "Provisional Government" tomorrow means that it has lost the Algerian war. For, in guerrilla conflicts, if you do not win you lose; there is no such thing as stalemate. The United States discovered this through its clients in Laos, and the British learned a similar lesson in Cyprus.

Only when partisan movements can be isolated and squashed, as in Greece and in Malaya, may real victory be claimed.

The French army, man for man the finest in the Western world, has isolated the rebels but it couldn't squash them. The first reason was that the nationalists had safe havens in Tunisia and Morocco which France's decency and world opinion kept jingo generals from attacking. The second reason was that both public sympathy among Algerian Moslems and history's tide favored the nationalist cause.

Thus, by sending a delegation to Evian to negotiate formally with the rebel "Government," France concedes reality to the insurrection and *de facto* recognition to its leadership. There can be no return from this position. The *status quo* has vanished.

It has vanished because de Gaulle wants peace, because he has largely disintegrated Right-wing political opposition to this wish, and because the professional officer corps which sought to contradict him was frustrated in its efforts. And this professional officer corps would have to fight the war produced by reversion to the *status quo*.

The question now is whether de Gaulle's wisdom and generosity will be shared. Will the rebels agree to a just basis for transition from war to peace, from subjection to independence? Will they be large and unbitter enough to make a fair life possible for the million non-Moslems who inhabit Algeria? This is the big issue. It transcends such burning matters as the future of the Sahara wasteland with its oil and de Gaulle's adamant insistence that France be granted base rights at rocky Mers-el-Kebir.

What is required, for the sake of the Moslem majority itself, which needs French economic and technical help, is a voluntary guarantee by the rebel leaders that anyone can be a free and equal citizen regardless of race or creed. This is the time for the "Provisional Government" to pledge to the minority precisely those rights within a free nation that the hitherto subjected majority has been claiming for itself.

Unfortunately, the problem has been confused by savagery for seven years. The French settlers in Algeria are decent people but their attachment to the land, their hankering for what de Gaulle calls "the Algeria of Papa," has led them to atavistic hatreds, more than reciprocated by the Moslems. The brain may dictate understanding to both sides; but it doesn't abate the passions of the heart.

For Europe, for Tunisia and Morocco, for NATO and for the United States one may hope these complex parleys will arrive at a solution that leads a free Algeria toward association with France and what we call democracy. For this is a destiny natural to the Western Mediterranean. And it is desired by many of the insurrection's chiefs. Nevertheless, the pressures against wisdom and restraint are heavy.

Russia is working both directly and through Cairo to urge the nationalists toward total break with France. Russia's family rival, China, favors war to the bitter end, the expulsion of all Frenchmen and French influence. And right below the top in the "Provisional Government" there is a vigorous anti-Western "Chinese" element.

Finally, on the other side, overshadowed but far from eliminated by de Gaulle, remains a rich, tough element in France and French Algeria, influential in the army, politics, and the business world, which will do anything to cling to the evaporating past. Anything includes another attempted *coup d'état,* assassination, mutiny, and even efforts to spread, not limit, the Algerian war.

One may hope lucidity will triumph over extremism on both sides. If not, one can foresee two desperate developments. The first would be renewed bloodshed, a leftward shift in the Algerian command, the end of Bourguiba's type of moderation, and that gradual Communization of North Africa which the French Right fears and stupidly abets. The second would be the fading in France of Gaullism and its replacement by chaos.

June 1961

Today's most serious diplomatic negotiation is that taking place at Evian-les-Bains, where French and Algerian nationalist envoys are seeking North African peace. On the outcome of their talks depend critical issues transcending Algeria in importance.

If the conference fails and the semi-interrupted war resumes, General de Gaulle may feel so frustrated that he might again retire from the active scene. If, on the other hand, they succeed he is likely to change his governing methods and work toward eventual installation of a Presidential system something like our own.

Both the future shape of France and the future shape of Africa are directly involved. An independent Algeria may eventually confederate with Tunisia and Morocco. Such a confederation would check Sino-Soviet aspirations and the kind of Arab nationalism fostered by Colonel Nasser by favoring Bourguiba's more moderate pro-Western policy.

NATO would be strengthened by Algerian peace. Ultimately the four French divisions earmarked for the alliance would be returned to Europe, thus bolstering defenses. And

France could speak in world councils with even greater influence as a leader in decolonializing.

One difficulty posed is the uncertainty of complete control by the nationalists' "Provisional Government" over all its guerrilla forces and political factions. Major Slimane of the Algerian delegation was involved in a curious affair last year when important rebel leaders sought a private truce with France. The chief among these, Si Salah, flew secretly to Paris, where he saw de Gaulle. He was later shot in a rebel purge costing almost five hundred lives among their troops. Slimane was in charge of the purge.

There are thus on both sides discordant elements working against the peace sought by their leaders. De Gaulle has reaffirmed his own authority in France after an unsuccessful coup and is disciplining his armed forces. Confidential instructions have even been disseminated among French units telling all ranks to report instances of disloyalty.

The global importance of the Algerian negotiation is immense. Should full-scale war resume, it is unlikely the conflict could remain isolated. The nationalists would virtually be forced to depend increasingly on the Communist bloc for aid. Yet, as General Norstad made clear two years ago in a memorandum:

"Until 1955 Algeria was a part of Allied command, Europe. It is still a part of NATO Europe, although not a part of my command. It is quite clear that it is a part of NATO and, if there were an external attack on Algeria, there would be a responsibility on the Alliance. I think such an attack would come quite clearly within the terms and the obligations of Article V of the treaty; there would be a NATO obligation in a case of external and active aggression against Algeria when Algeria is a part of the NATO area."

It requires no great foresight to perceive ugly international clouds gathering should the Evian talks collapse. One may therefore pray that the nationalists will recognize the genuineness of de Gaulle's efforts to bring peace to Algeria, despite the great risks these efforts pose to his own power and prestige. This is the time for fair compromise in a generous spirit.

July 1961

Once when discussing the intricate Algerian problem, General de Gaulle remarked: "Suppose you in the United States had a population of forty million Redskins. This fact would have to be recognized. You would have to acknowledge their religion and their rights. You could not force them to become Christian and to change their status. You must think of things in this way with respect to Algeria's demography."

The French President was not referring, in this simile, to the Algerian majority of Berber and Arab Moslems. It used to be fashionable among cynical, tough European settlers to compare these with American Indians and to add brutally: "You in the U.S.A. were smart enough to kill most of them off."

On the contrary, de Gaulle was referring to the French minority so heavily outnumbered in the Algeria of the future he would help create. He wants to insure this minority's well-being in an independent state which, he still hopes, can be linked in friendly association with France.

The recently interrupted peace negotiations at Evian-les-Bains never developed beyond the stage of a repetitious diplomatic phonograph. At a point where it seemed there might be serious bargaining, the rebels deadlocked discussions.

One cannot be entirely sure just why the rebel "Provisional Government" seemed so anxious to stalemate the Evian talks. It is possible the rebels thought they could do better later. It is possible that they felt France's recalcitrant army and angry farmers might weaken de Gaulle's position. Or it is possible that promises of future help were given by the Communist bloc if the rebels kept the French tied up until this autumn's Berlin crisis.

Whatever the reason, it is obvious de Gaulle has no intention of yielding to rebel convenience in the timing of a just peace protecting all segments of the population. If the nationalists refuse to get down to business, he has a valuable trump card to play, the trump that is called partition.

Partition of Algeria would be insane. Nobody really wants it. Hundreds of thousands of Europeans and pro-French Moslems would have to be moved to a coastal strip from west of Oran to west of Bougie and hundreds of thousands of pronationalist Arabs and Berbers would have to be expelled.

What would be created is a kind of French "Israel" surrounded by another hostile, Arab hinterland. This is one sure way of perpetuating the Algerian war and, eventually, of internationalizing it by bringing in Arab League and possibly Communist-bloc support. Everybody would lose. The French enclave in Algeria would include Maison Blanche airbase and Mers-el-Kebir naval base and would be militarily easy to defend with limited troops. It would be an unsatisfactory long-term solution but could work—just as Cyprus's independence formula was unsatisfactory but workable.

The fact of the matter is that de Gaulle has no desire for

this solution. He had studied the partition of India and Palestine and has seen how much trouble they produced. This is not his idea for Algeria and, one may assume, he will do everything reasonably possible to avoid it.

But he doesn't intend to be diddled along by the rebels. If they are not prepared to negotiate seriously, as de Gaulle has shown himself ready to do despite political difficulties, he has no desire to wait. He would prefer an imperfect solution now rather than a more perfect solution later. And, de Gaulle reasons: "In the end the Algerians will find they need France far more than France needs them."

SEVEN

The Final Conspiracy

July 1961

For swagger, audacity, and ardor, the French army is the finest in the West. Parisians who watched it parade down the Champs Elysées on this Bastille Day took pride in the reminder of splendid military traditions. Nevertheless, fanfare, drum rattles, and the quick-stepping march could not entirely obscure the fact that France's army is a bitterly divided force whose future is an uncertain factor in this country's destiny.

By giving France strong government de Gaulle has prevented the army from making revolution—but not for lack of trying. And few people regarding today's magnificent display could fail to note glaring absences. Since last spring's abortive *Putsch,* the army has been disciplined and purged. Its famous S.A.S., or Special Services, have been reorganized. Three parachute regiments, including one from the Foreign Legion, have been dissolved as well as three air commandos noted for panache.

Three generals and five renowned colonels are fugitives and plotting again to oust the Gaullist regime. Six generals are in prison and others have been relieved of their commands. One hundred and ninety officers are under fortress arrest and fourteen have been degraded. Furthermore, Alphonse-Pierre Juin, the nation's only living Field Marshal, openly indicates sympathy with this infractious group.

Once again rumors circulate that another uprising is being planned for late July or August. The O.A.S. asks Europeans in Algeria to be ready for a sudden "mobilization."

The Secret Army Organization, whose slogan is "French Algeria or Death," issues pronunciamentos signed by Generals Salan and Jouhaud, two of the four leaders in the unsuccessful April coup. Both men, under death sentence, are hiding in Algeria. They are supported by two of France's best-known officers, Colonels Yves Godard and Jean Gardes, who recently consulted secretly with a Moslem colonel, Si Chérif, commander of a French army Moslem unit. Moslem troops or *harkis* serving France see that the future for them is dim in an independent Algeria.

There is no way of knowing the answers to two vital questions. The first is: How extensive and important is the O.A.S.? The second is: Does it really plan another coup and when? Since the great mass of metropolitan Frenchmen back de Gaulle's Algerian policy, he could probably squash any new uprising as effectively as he did the last.

For not only does he remain a tower of strength; there is no military leader evident who could command a serious mutiny without contest and seek to defy the Government. Furthermore, the draftees commanded by the disgruntled professional officer corps are loyal to de Gaulle; many conscripts have transistor radios on which they heard the President order them to disregard mutinous chieftains. This helped destroy last April's *Putsch*.

Though France's security services have been unable to track down the main plotters, de Gaulle appears confident he has shattered the network of schemers. He has even begun to draw troops from Algeria to build up NATO strength for a Berlin crisis. The President's bland assurance implies that nerve-racking O.A.S. pamphlets and the organization's plastic-bomb outrages are psychological but not material threats.

By sheer force of personality de Gaulle has publicly proven his belief that France's army is not a political power. But how about after de Gaulle? In the end the Fifth Republic will be judged by its success in accomplishing this task, in proving to future Bastille Day spectators that the army on parade is their servant, not an aspiring master.

September 1961

Among professional officers at the head of O.A.S. are four generals and four colonels who served in Indochina and were deeply affected by that tragic conflict. They were instrumental in arranging that Mao Tse-tung's writings be required reading at the Ecole Militaire six years ago. These officers, and dozens of others like them who sought to elaborate a new doctrine of revolutionary or subversive war, in no way endorsed Communism's philosophical concepts. Indeed, they tended increasingly toward Right-wing ideas. But they tried to use the operational methods of Communism for their own purposes, first in Algeria and later in France itself.

The techniques stemmed from the Vietminh handbook called *Guerrilla Warfare According to the Communist School* and became available to the French when it was republished by Belgian Congo military authorities seven years ago. These techniques were précised by French military intellectuals in 1956 and 1957. The five steps to success were thus defined:

(1) Trained agents infiltrate an area, begin preparation of the political terrain, gather secret discussion and agitation groups, locate sources of discontent, and find personnel to build a Politico-Administrative Organization, or O.P.A.

(2) This organizes the population into political groupings under O.P.A. surveillance and begins to infiltrate existing gov-

ernmental authority. Rudimentary terror cells are started.

(3) The terror begins with efforts to menace or kill members of the existing governmental authority and to instill fear.

(4) Local O.P.A. leadership is established in selected zones and an effort is made to recruit for its armed forces.

(5) A general psychological and military offensive begins and this seeks to elicit foreign support.

In one or another way such techniques were tried by the French army against its Algerian nationalist opponents. They infiltrated rebel ranks and civilian areas; they armed discontented Moslems in groups called *harkas* and in deviationist bands; they tried to create rival administrative organizations, to establish "free" areas, to regroup population, and to kill individual rebel leaders.

But they failed in the end because these techniques ignored Mao's first lesson:

"If the political objectives that one seeks to attain are not the secret and profound aspirations of the masses, all is lost from the beginning."

All, in the sense of real victory, was therefore lost in Algeria. The resulting frustration among professional officers, French settlers, and some pro-French Algerians caused certain officers and extremist politicians to form the O.A.S.

But the O.A.S., since its inception this year, no longer limited itself to efforts at conquering Algeria. It began to dream of conquering France. It had its men among the conspirators who tried to upset the Fifth Republic last spring. It is believed to have had its men in the recent endeavor to murder de Gaulle—although the O.A.S. denies this.

The O.A.S. would like to apply the five steps of *la guerre révolutionnaire* in the mother country.

But what was folly in Algeria becomes madness in France. The O.A.S. has been trying to use revolutionary techniques designed to express popular aspirations in an attempt to achieve counterrevolution opposing popular aspirations. The French nation wants de Gaulle and Algerian peace. It doesn't want the O.A.S.

Therefore, the O.A.S. is not only cruel but insane in hoping to upset the national equilibrium by killing its symbol. That could only produce chaos. The O.A.S. might hope to benefit from such chaos and place its henchmen in power. But they could not remain there long, because the majority of Frenchmen would not accept them. In a pinch they might well, if forced, turn Left rather than Right.

The Communists know this. The danger of using revolutionary tactics to seek counterrevolution is that they will result in the thing most feared—revolution itself. This is true logic—whether the O.A.S. acknowledges it or not.

October 1961

"The war in Algeria will end some time between October 31 this year and October 31, 1962." This flat prediction was made to me some months ago by one of France's highest-ranking generals, a man renowned in an army of divided loyalties for his allegiance to President de Gaulle.

The General argued that civil wars have a habit of lasting seven years—a fact denied by history if supported by astrology—and that one must wait for the seventh year to finish before the Algerian cancer can be healed. The seventh year ends on Tuesday, anniversary of the first uprising in the Aures Mountains.

Of course, this categorical clairvoyance is founded on illogic. But, as is so often the case in France, illogic may well triumph. One thing is assuredly certain: De Gaulle's Fifth Republic will be tested sorely during the next twelve months and its definitive fate is likely to be settled.

The signs of approaching crisis multiply. While the Algerian rebel leadership continues secret contacts with de Gaulle in preparation, it is hoped, for another round of peace talks, anti-Gaullist conspirators in both France and Algeria prepare another effort to upset the Paris Government, and bloody riots are now commonplace on both Mediterranean shores.

Since July the O.A.S. has been perfecting plots. It seeks to attract both military and civilian support, to spread clandestine and open propaganda, to encourage terrorism and to scheme political murder.

Coded broadcasts and coded letters crisscross France. *Verdun,* in reality a dissident general, writes to *Claude,* a colonel in hiding, about intrigues against *Grande Zora,* President de Gaulle himself. The "Three G's," colonels at the top of the O.A.S. command, have eluded all efforts to arrest them. The O.A.S. has even penetrated the Defense and Interior Ministries and stolen classified General Staff documents.

Once again the professional army corps, shaken by last April's abortive *Putsch* and the sentencing of five generals, is torn by dissent. One by one, top commanders leave the services. Four generals, including the French representative on NATO's Standing Group, retired voluntarily in September. The Chief of Staff, now on temporary leave, will finally resign Wednesday.

For more than three years elements among the professional officers have been in sullen opposition to the state.

On May 23, 1958, General Salan, in Algeria, prepared an airborne assault (called Operation Resurrection) against the dying Fourth Republic, an assault to be aided by a co-ordinated paratroop rebellion in Toulouse.

Last April he planned a similar move, to be helped by French army units in central France and Germany. And now he is somewhere in Algeria, planning yet another coup. His agents have so successfully penetrated Government security forces that he continually eludes capture.

Salan is a silly man and the leadership of his movement is muddled. Nevertheless, it is plain they intend a new *Putsch,* this time to establish an "independent" and "European" Algerian state on the seacoast between Algiers and Oran.

January 1962

Franco-American relations are at their lowest ebb since World War II, although, paradoxically, this does not mean they are in essence bad. An immense reservoir of good will exists but relations have deteriorated steadily since President Kennedy's spring Paris visit.

That visit ended with General de Gaulle grasping his guest's hand and saying: "I have more confidence in your country now." Informal understanding was reached that the U.S. would henceforth fully consult the French on major policy. Mr. Kennedy explained our reluctance to increase the number of militarily atomic nations and therefore give France nuclear help. Each felt he understood the other on Berlin.

The Franco-American mood was excellent when Mr. Kennedy flew off to Vienna and Khrushchev's cold-water douche. But that mood has changed. There has been mounting despair in Washington as the new Administration learned how stubborn de Gaulle can be, and there has been cold irritation in Paris at our Berlin and U.N. tactics.

Old French frustrations express themselves in pinpricks. Private sneers are directed at U.S. officials. And thwarted intellectuals writing in the liberal press, often with more wind than wisdom, develop Fidel Castro as a kind of Left Bank, Left-wing hothouse pet with which to torment Uncle Sam.

French participation in NATO remains that of cold war cobelligerent, not ally. One tends to forget that France's fleet is outside NATO, that the position of French naval deputy at SHAPE has long been vacant. De Gaulle brought two divisions back from Algeria and two more will come this year; but they are not assigned to NATO. The French air force is not co-ordinated in allied air defense. De Gaulle has never visited SHAPE, some twelve miles from Paris.

President Kennedy has made numerous efforts to explain United States policy to General de Gaulle, to consult him and to elicit his views. Some of these efforts can be discussed because they already belong to history.

Mr. Kennedy invited the French President to join him and Mr. Macmillan in a Western summit some seven weeks before his Bermuda talk with the British Prime Minister. He had originally hoped that not only de Gaulle but also Chancellor Adenauer could attend; but the General was disinterested.

Likewise, during the unfortunate December NATO meeting, Mr. Kennedy personally telephoned de Gaulle to ask him to withdraw his blanket opposition to any form of negotiation with Khrushchev on Berlin. With William Tyler, State Department expert and brilliant linguist, sitting beside him and interpreting, the President explained the U.S. position. Nevertheless France's Foreign Minister was later instructed to warn that if the word "negotiated" was even mentioned in the Council's communiqué, there would be no communiqué—an impasse settled only after bitter argument.

This kind of interallied difference understandably irks some of the State Department and Pentagon officials. The President, however, has wisely displayed calm and restraint. He shows polite understanding of the French attitude, or, at any rate, of what it is now compounded.

The important thing to remember is that France at this instant is on the verge of painful convulsion. Within a relatively short time the final process of ending the long Algerian war will start. It is almost bound to involve bloodshed. The instant the rebels' "Government" accepts the formula de Gaulle now offers, dissident French army elements will rise.

As a result, France is in a somewhat psychotic condition. Politically it is almost schizoid, withdrawn from world reality, and also, as a nation, paranoiacally suspicious and sensitive. Furthermore, this nation has been curiously split into segments. The politically active and intellectual leaders, concentrated in Paris, are largely divided both from de Gaulle and from the passive majority in the hinterland.

One must add to this the well-known fact that General de Gaulle is always most obstinate when he feels himself weak. Today, as the crucial test with both the Algerian rebels and the insurrectional O.A.S. looms, his position is uncertain. It cannot be re-established until the test has been met.

For these reasons it would be well for all Washington officials meticulously to follow Mr. Kennedy's lead and continue to exercise sympathetic patience toward America's oldest ally in what will shortly be its great travail.

My considered guess is that there will either be an Algerian peace agreement between France and the rebel National Liberation Front within a month or there will be disaster in Algeria and possibly in France itself.

During more than seven years many oracular reputations have been staked and lost on this sad and sanguinary issue. Nevertheless, today cruel logic brings the drama toward its inescapable denouement.

Secret negotiations, accelerated in the last three weeks, have attained a point where it is almost possible to foresee the independence of an Algerian state. This would, however, insure France certain military base rights, economic and cultural guarantees, including the promise that Algeria would remain in the franc zone and that French would be a recognized language, like English in India.

Nevertheless, both sides are negotiating on the premise of a bet. The French gamble that the three principal leaders of the F.L.N. Provisional Government are strong enough to carry out pledges they make, despite opposition elements in their ranks.

The Algerian rebels gamble that General de Gaulle's Government can enforce any compact signed upon a nervous officer corps, an aroused European minority in Algeria, and on the desperate O.A.S.

The French are betting on Benyoussef Ben Khedda, Premier; and Saad Dahlab, Foreign Minister in the rebel Cabinet. The Algerians are betting on de Gaulle.

Since autumn there have been bargaining concessions on both sides. The French no longer seek to divide the Sahara and its oil from the rest of Algeria. They agree to a referendum this year to decide all the area's fate.

The F.L.N. likewise at last acknowledges certain French base rights, above all naval installations at Mers-el-Kebir, that French investments would be safeguarded, and the franc would remain currency. Nevertheless, a free Algeria would probably pursue a policy tinged with neutralism and socialism.

The big questions still under discussion are: How would a joint French-F.L.N. administration of Algeria be managed during the final phase-out? And how many non-Moslems would be accepted as citizens of an independent state?

The latter issue is primordial. The French insist that anyone now living in Algeria should be accepted as a future citizen. The F.L.N. insists that each must specifically voice a desire to remain—hoping to reduce the total. Extremist pressures could prevent most Europeans from opting for Algeria under this formula.

Paris desires an accord on an Algeria associated with France and in which all non-Moslems would have complete rights. Such an accord would almost surely deprive the O.A.S. of its main popular support. But if the accord is not adequately precise, popular support of non-Moslems will remain behind the O.A.S. insuring *de facto* partition and violence.

The F.L.N. has problems vis-à-vis its own diehard minority. Nevertheless, if the ruling triumvirate doesn't soon take the risk of meeting the French on the primordial issue, the prospect of settlement may explode.

Today France's civilian administration of Algeria is half paralyzed and only the army really represents Paris. This army has risen against the Government before, but de Gaulle reckons he can still rely on it. That assumption will not be valid indefinitely if peace is not soon achieved.

The O.A.S. is hard-bitten and skilled in conspiracy. It

now faces three choices. It could resign itself to the inevitable, the desire of most Frenchmen to end the terrible war. It could rise up in violence when an accord is announced. Or it could deliberately revolt after assassinations in France and accompanied by proclamation of its own "independent" state, probably around the bitter city of Oran. Violence increases daily. Rumors grow. Last week an abortive attack was mounted against de Gaulle's Algerian administrative headquarters.

The bell has begun to toll, a bell whose sound bodes fatefully for tormented Algeria, for the sweet land of France, and for NATO and the West.

If the O.A.S. thinks bravado will scare de Gaulle from his intention of signing a peace with the rebel Algerian National Liberation Front and from ordering his army to enforce any such pact, the O.A.S. is wrong. As France's allies know, General de Gaulle is an unyieldingly obstinate man. France's enemies, including the O.A.S., should also know this.

Parisians had already been upset by O.A.S. plastic bombing and reports of O.A.S. coups among officer sympathizers before the Quai d'Orsay incident, the bombing of the Foreign Ministry. De Gaulle himself is not impressed. He remains disdainfully confident that the course he seeks is correct.

He brooks no opposition. He is certain that if he must command his army to defend order in Algeria or France, the army will defend order—despite conspiratorial elements. He feels the influence of the O.A.S. in France itself is nil—that not 20,000 Frenchmen endorse it; that inside Algeria, if he commands his country's forces to move, they will move.

For him the question of Algeria's future is not something

to be settled by France's Government, or by the O.A.S. conspiracy. It must now, in the last analysis, be settled by the F.L.N. leadership, which agrees on the principal terms of peace but still refuses to sign a cease-fire.

Today he feels it is up to the F.L.N. to assume responsibility; to deal as a government and not as a set of clan chiefs; to accept the peace already negotiated in broad principal. France waits.

If the F.L.N. does not accept, France will unilaterally impose a temporary solution. It will begin what is called the policy of regroupment. It will squeeze European settlers from the hinterland into areas around such towns as Algiers, Oran, and Bône; and it will squeeze Moslem Algerians out.

De Gaulle plays the O.A.S. and the F.L.N. against each other. His Government is in no sense allied with the F.L.N. But it sees its aspiration for independence as valid in this age of decolonization.

French intellectuals sometimes describe General de Gaulle as a man of decision, not action. This is the kind of aphorism peculiarly appealing to the Gallic mind, endowed more with the appearance of profundity than profundity itself.

It implies that while de Gaulle decided to grant independence to Algeria, he has done nothing to apply his decision; that he sits in isolation, removed from the tumult that engulfs Algerian cities and the terror that creeps into France, disdainful of the burbling tremors of fear and conspiracy that seem to threaten this superficially placid land. De Gaulle has held power forty-four months with unprecedented authority. Plebiscites have shown he is backed by most Frenchmen in his determination to end the Algerian war. Yet, today, part of his officer corps is in open insurrection through the O.A.S.;

peace has not embraced Algeria, where anarchic race war prevails; and murder, kidnaping, desertions, and bombing intrude into France itself.

One must delve below the surface, however, and there one finds other facts. Negotiations with the Algerian rebels have reached the point where peace can be declared tomorrow if only the F.L.N. will sign. And the actual war has changed its nature. In large areas French troops have been or are being withdrawn and a kind of complaisant co-administration exists between the French and the F.L.N.

The Algerian fury with its sanguinary ramifications is now concentrated in a few key regions, primarily around large towns. In those regions there are today three, not two, belligerents: Moslem Algerians tied to the F.L.N.; France's army and officialdom; and European Algerians, banded behind an O.A.S last stand.

Because hatred is geographically constricted, this phase of the tragedy is the most frightening. Secret fortresses have been established inside these final strongholds by both F.L.N. and O.A.S. commandos, while French administrators have withdrawn to peripheral points.

This is not the result of any *laisser-aller* attitude of de Gaulle. What he is doing with cold calculation is to impose a partial and temporary solution which will ultimately change the balance of forces—unless the O.A.S. can win France's army to its side. De Gaulle is sure it cannot.

De Gaulle is already putting into effect his policy of what he calls regroupment, concentration of European Algerians into certain coastal sectors. This forces many of them to decide to quit the bloody land for France—despite O.A.S. threats against such emigration. And de Gaulle is slowly withdrawing his army.

Inch by inch, in an atmosphere of horror—more intense

because more localized—de Gaulle is acting, is squeezing both size and shape of an amorphous war. It is becoming a city civil war instead of a country guerrilla campaign.

De Gaulle would prefer the F.L.N. to help in achieving settlement by signing the terms before it. But the F.L.N. wonders if de Gaulle can apply those terms in the face of O.A.S. terror. He thinks he can, that the army will execute any commands he gives. But he will give no commands until the Moslem rebels sign.

As for the O.A.S., today *de facto* ruler of most Algerian Europeans, de Gaulle considers it unimportant in France, despite its crimes, and not a political reality in Algeria, only an emotional reality. If the F.L.N. accepts his peace terms, he thinks many European Algerians will shake free of O.A.S. discipline and isolate what he considers a "tedious" movement.

February 1962

Since his youth, de Gaulle has chosen to separate himself from usual human contacts while pursuing a lonely path. He felt he might be selected for a special destiny which could best be achieved by a solitary leader. This did not mean for him isolation from reality in the form of history's tides or basic national needs. But these, he evidently calculated, must be seen from the viewpoint of grandeur.

Reality and grandeur are the keys to his character. He admires the classicists who had grandeur, for "that has always been my taste." He also admires history's effective men, *"les gens efficaces,"* who faced trouble and surmounted it. Choosing grandeur as both technique and aim, he nevertheless reckoned a man may only be measured by what he accomplishes, that everything else is fiction.

In music and in literature one finds the romantic in de Gaulle's private tastes: Beethoven more than Mozart; Debussy, Delibes; Schumann and Schubert; and, at moments, Wagner; Corneille, Racine, Chateaubriand, Hugo, Goethe.

In philosophy and biography, one sees the more realistic strain: Bergson and Comte; Clovis, Charlemagne, Henri IV; Clemenceau, Jefferson, Theodore Roosevelt, Bismarck; even Bismarck, despite the harm he did France.

De Gaulle is frequently accused of being an autocrat, which he surely is by manner, but he is also a republican. Before he departs he wishes to stiffen this Republic, to endow it with enduring strength. That does not mean he intends to install a presidential system, modeled on our own, with a chief of state who doubles as chief of government and carries a vice-presidential spare tire. De Gaulle is evidently content with the essentials of the present structure.

He regards it as essential to have a President orienting fundamental policy and a Premier dealing with diurnal events. All he would like is to have his successor chosen by direct universal suffrage—instead of the present more restricted means—to insure the next President's popular authority.

Such ideas, still nebulous, belong to a future which is also nebulous until the Algerian battle ends. In the meantime Frenchmen point out the apparent contradiction between de Gaulle's determination to abandon Algeria and his determination to do it in the name of French grandeur. But grandeur may refer to greatness of character as well as greatness of power.

The task de Gaulle has set himself is to refurbish the romantic aspect of the former even at what might appear to be the expense of the latter's reality. But in this world of superstates, the latter's reality is but a romance after all.

EIGHT

Down with Intelligence; Long Live Death!

February 1962

Secret negotiations with the Algerian nationalists have been hovering for weeks on the verge of accord. But an invisible question affects the French gamble. This is: Will a treaty with the existing F.L.N. Government imply any sort of permanent political relationship with a future free Algeria? Or will this be upset by further revolution? The case of Egypt, underscored by its ninth republican anniversary, is remembered. Naguib's Government, which ousted King Farouk, was respected by the West and regarded as a friend. Yet Naguib was the symbol of change, not the reality. He was soon eased out by the more vibrant Nasser and has since been a virtual prisoner, provided with pleasant food and drink and carefully kept from sight.

Nasser's more strident nationalism replaced the quiet, conservative Naguib approach, which concentrated on purifying the existing situation rather than overturning it. What, the French ask, will become of the Algerian leaders with whom they now negotiate?

This group, headed by Benyoussef Ben Khedda, Belkacem Krim, and Saad Dahlab, is broadly considered pro-French and pro-Western, if clearly nationalistic. And this group is presently selected by the F.L.N. to represent it in peace parleys. What would happen, however, if, after peace is signed, the relatively sympathetic leaders were replaced by others of antagonistic views?

There are important Algerian rebels who detest the West and others unabashedly sympathetic to Communism, especially Chinese Communism. They have closer connections with Peiping than with Moscow. There has been distaste for Western Communism ever since a Paris Government, including two Communist ministers, squashed an Algerian revolt after World War II.

Paris, realistically aware of this imponderable, will be trying to guide its diplomacy along a line of built-in insurance. This accepts the possibility that an eventual free Algerian Government may be neutralist.

The French therefore want guarantees on the following points: (1) Algeria will remain in the franc fiscal zone; (2) there will be economic condominium over the oil-filled Sahara region; (3) French presence on military bases will be pledged for a fixed time; (4) there will be adequate safeguards for non-Moslems, hitherto called "French."

These are reasonable demands. No matter what benevolence may be entertained by the F.L.N. triumvirate with which de Gaulle now negotiates, there is no assurance it will stay forever in control of the heady revolutionary movement.

The only Algerian, perhaps, with the potential dynamic authority of a Bourguiba is Mohammed Ben Bella, now a French prisoner. And no one can predict what Ben Bella's views or influence will be when he is liberated.

For these reasons France, while seeking Algerian peace, finds itself in the peculiar position of negotiating with a Naguib while looking over history's shoulder for a Nasser.

Destiny played a bitter joke on France by hiding the rich Saharan oil and gas pool until the French were already being pushed from this area by Arab nationalism's tide.

Now, after a few years of arduous work, just as the first bloom begins on the harsh and endless desert, a knell sounds for change. A peace treaty between Paris and the Algerian rebels will, when signed, give the rebels political control of the broad Sahara.

Until almost yesterday this was an impoverished, hopeless, barren region of feudal oasis societies and nomadic tribes. But today one sees the vision of a different future, symbolized by drilling rigs.

Profits from petroleum and natural gas are being pumped into the wasteland. Airstrips, roads, and buildings blossom where once there was only sand. A dream of French energy comes true economically just as, politically, it proves to be another cruel mirage.

Once again we see our era's immutable trend: northward the course of empire takes its way, northward and backward, retreating into time. And France, in a splendid imperial death throe, builds feverishly on the eve of its departure.

It seems a curious rule for empires, as they end, to start ambitious projects benefiting those who oust them. This has been true of Britain and of Belgium. Now, in both Algeria and the Sahara, it becomes the case with France.

The incipient Algerian state should see the logic of asking the French to continue these developments, a privilege indeed to be assured by treaty. Will treaties be honored? Logic dictates the need for French skill, experience, and capital. But logic does not always prevail.

The conflict hardly impinged upon the Saharan wilderness. There is an air of confident hustle and tranquillity in new plants and old oasis towns. But underneath is a current of unease. No one pretends to know precisely what the future holds: Frenchman, Arab, Berber, or Mozabite. The only thing certain is uncertainty and over the horizon lie dim and frightening images.

Whatever occurs, there is no doubt France will persevere as a vibrant nation. One need only remember that five of the six European Common Market lands—all save Luxembourg—were once imperial powers. And all but France have already shed virtually every imperial appanage.

Yet these countries have actually become healthier and more prosperous as their pretensions shrank upon the map. Withdrawn from the earth's corners and constricted in narrow confines, the energies that once made empires now are making a new industrial revolution.

In the imperial wake we see oddly contradictory developments on the neighbor continents of Europe and Africa. The former colonies of Africa burst with nationalism, which, unless it is controlled, may embroil them in other types of war as they seek to colonize each other. But the former empires of Europe edge along a different path. Gradually they abandon nationalism and confederate the talents that hitherto they sent abroad.

These diverging regions nevertheless still need each other. What is slowly becoming a supranationalist Europe requires the neonationalist desert's fuel. And if Algeria's coming leaders do not also recognize their dependence on Europe's help and wealth, the sands may once again sweep over the Sahara.

On paper this fact is acknowledged by the statesmen now in or near Switzerland punctuating the terms of Algerian peace. But the emotions that have gone into this latest, longest African conflict are not spent. Wild anger still rumbles between possessed and dispossessed.

The final task, which in the end will prove the most important, is to arrange a marriage of convenience, a wedding between the eager and backward young lands that have now seized liberty and the wise old countries that gave it to them. Otherwise and ultimately it will be hard for either to progress without the other.

Therefore the sooner reason and generosity replace the residue of passion that always remains after the rough process of freedom, the better it will be for all. So much is evident, but how often emotion is allowed to obscure the clarity of truth.

The key words used by French security forces guarding murderous Algiers are "Chicago" and "Albatross." When the short-wave radio linking patrol cars and their fortified headquarters flashes an "*Alerte* Chicago," this means a gunning or bombing incident. "Albatross" is code for the security command itself. Thus, "Albatross, Albatross, *alerte* Chicago" is a sign of trouble.

Chicago, in French fancy, signifies a kind of movie gangster's shooting gallery. But more people in Algiers die violently each day than in the Midwestern city's gaudiest era. Censored newspapers merely list such incidents in a laconic column entitled "crimes of violence." Thursday there were twenty-four.

I do not know the origin of "Albatross" in the police code, but it is apt. For Algiers today hangs around the neck of France like the festering bird borne by Coleridge's Ancient Mariner.

On the surface this well-sited, well-built town is one of the loveliest on the Mediterranean. On clear days the sun gleams and the athletic *Algérois* lounge along the waterfront.

The wistaria is out. Pigeons flutter among children playing in the squares.

Despite the tragedy that stalks and sometimes explodes in savagery, there is an aspect of tranquil laziness. Men and women idle on the sidewalks. Then one realizes with astonishment that everything, shops, restaurants, cafés, has been closed by a strike. Once again the O.A.S. has shut down the capital to show its strength.

Before the seat of France's administration, now largely deserted in favor of a suburban stronghold, there is an armored car park that would do credit to a city occupied in war. Soldiers stand guard, clutching tommy guns, or pick their way slowly down the streets with that special, meticulously dainty Gallic military step, like young foxes.

You regard this scene, which has become so ordinary that it strangely lacks in nervousness, and then your companion says, pointing along the crowded avenue: "In the last four months at least one person has been murdered on every corner you can see from here."

Nowadays there is less bombing and more pistoling of victims, which adds to the leaden atmosphere of quiet. And after nine o'clock the nights are silent. For the French authorities who try to administer this sullen place have fixed a curfew. When it sets in only those cars granted special permits are allowed to circulate. But the O.A.S. considers such vehicles, favored by the Paris Government, fair targets for its roof-top snipers.

So people sit home plotting or brooding on these silent nights. They have stocked up food and drink because the O.A.S. commanded them to do so. They lift their glasses in grim toasts when the quiet is sometimes punctuated by a bang.

Algiers is no city of crime in the Chicago cinematic sense. Blood is shed for causes. The Moslem kills for "liberty"; the European Algerian, to hold his position; the French gendarme, in the name of order. And what is now called *"la saison du hold-up,"* when banks and tills are robbed, is for the purpose of filling revolutionary treasuries.

North Africa's "Chicago" is no ordinary gangland with its Jake the Barber as a French boss, its Scarface Al of the O.A.S., or its Moslem mob. These are serious men, all of whom, although they call each other traitors, earnestly believe in the rightness of their causes.

The time of troubles that has embraced Algiers is the culmination of a long historic movement. It began two generations ago with the Arab revolt in the Middle East and now its last agonies have constricted around this littoral where Frenchmen settled more than a century earlier and fight desperately to stay.

At last the final test begins. The O.A.S. seems to believe with Oswald Spengler that "in the last resort it has always been a platoon of soldiers who have saved civilization."

But this platoon is squeezed in a cruel, tightening vise.

For, from all the Continent of Africa, history's wave presses up against it. And, in the North, the people of prosperous France want to shed the burden of the albatross. Can a "platoon" turn history? No.

Like other conspiratorial movements, the O.A.S. is relatively small in active membership, a few thousand. Its civilian dogmatist, Jean-Jacques Susini, is preoccupied with Algeria, which he would probably like to turn into a kind of Socialist-corporative state. Its military chieftains, headed by General Salan, seem more concerned with changing the Government in France itself. Susini is in hiding in Algiers and Salan less than thirty miles away. Their colleague, General Jouhaud, is in bloody and insane Oran.

These leaders do not always agree. One insurrectional general recently wrote another civilian leader, warning that if Soustelle, the pro-O.A.S. French politician, should come here, he would have him shot. But internal differences are submerged in the combined cause of keeping Moslem nationalists from control of Algeria and trying to unseat de Gaulle.

The O.A.S. pretends Algerian independence would subject this country to Russian influence. It denounces de Gaulle as advocating war, dictatorship, and Communism. It proclaims: "Neither suitcase nor coffin," meaning neither emigration nor defeat, and "one gun, one country." It boasts it "strikes where it wants, when it wants, whom it wants."

The O.A.S. declared "total war and general mobilization" January 4, although announcing this mobilization was *sur place,* as in the Israeli and Swiss armies and the anarchist federation of Spain's Civil War. These comparisons are designed to appeal to French, Spanish, and Jewish supporters.

Some time ago it was thought Salan planned a *Putsch* when a cease-fire is announced between de Gaulle and the Algerian nationalists. Now he says there will be no *Putsch,* merely a steady increase in disrupting strikes, murders, bombings, and gradual seizure of real power.

But despite effective organizational methods, the O.A.S. is founded less on reality than other similar movements. It is opposed by opinion in Africa and Europe and by the wave of history. Except by assassination, it cannot dislodge de Gaulle. Nor could a rump "French Algerian" state long survive.

The O.A.S. is not backed by foreign support, as was true

of the Jewish revolutionists in Palestine, or unanimous local sentiment, as was true of Ireland's I.R.A. Even among Algeria's frightened Europeans there have been voices raised in protest against its brutality. The local Archbishop Léon-Etienne Duval sadly urges this community "never to have recourse to unjust violence."

In hysterical Algiers where it is, believe it or not, no unfamiliar sight to see a man kicked to death, one talks with few Europeans who are not ardently pro-O.A.S. But when they develop their logic, they disclose ideas of the outside world that resemble the distortions of a Coney Island mirror.

The psychological result resembles that described by Algeria's greatest writer, Albert Camus, who said about an imaginary plague in Oran: "We had nothing left but the past, and even if some were tempted to live in the future, they had speedily to abandon the idea."

Many O.A.S. adherents, apart from paid assassins or fanatics, are decent people who oppose what they consider unreasoning injustice. But they are both blind and doomed. Conspiratorial movements must, to stand a chance of success, use harsh methods. But this one is founded on a memory, not a dream.

It slowly backs itself into an intellectual corner of unreality. Its slogan might well be that favorite motto of the Spanish Foreign Legion: "Down with intelligence; long live death."

Previously there have been four officers' attempts to unseat de Gaulle's Fifth Republic. In October 1959, Generals Salan, Jouhaud, and Zeller made a stillborn effort. Salan and Jouhaud are now hiding in Algeria; Zeller is in prison.

In January 1960, the "barricades" uprising exploded prematurely. In December 1960, there was another abortive try at winning army support for Salan. Last April, General Challe joined the original generals' triumvirate and ended up in jail. We are now witnessing the fifth and gravest plot.

In the sense of doctrine as well as improved conspiratorial techniques the Secret Army Organization of General Salan differs from previous insurrectional groups. Among its leaders, under surveillance in Spain's Canary Islands, is Colonel Charles Lacheroy, author of *A Lesson in Revolutionary Warfare*.

To the lessons learned in Indochina they add their own interpretations of Russian studies on mass psychology by the physiologist Ivan Pavlov and by Serge Tchakotine, who, as a refugee in France, wrote *The Rape of the Masses* before he returned to Moscow, where he is now a professor.

French academies have heard officers like Lacheroy teach how to "conquer strength with weakness." They have been told—inaccurately—that this century has seen twenty-one "revolutionary" wars of which eleven have failed.

French interpretation of "revolutionary warfare" insists a decisive test must be avoided until insurrectionists are ready to strike with maximum force. The first or "pre-insurrectional" phase concentrates on: selective terrorism, intimidation, threats of assassination, "intoxication," and "elimination" of opposing leaders.

The O.A.S., although stepping up its assault, still considers itself in this "pre-insurrectional" stage. It is murdering opponents, intimidating with plastic bombs, and seeking to "intoxicate" the non-Moslem masses of Algeria and the excitable and romantic elements among French university students.

For some months—and with some success—the O.A.S. has sought to follow *Revolutionary Warfare*'s precept of keeping the adversary blind—that is to say, unaware of its true strength. Paris has so far failed to launch a useful and massive counterpropaganda effort.

In the meantime, the O.A.S. has prepared for the moment when it will choose to strike and has accelerated its program of murder, terror, accumulation of stolen uniforms, weapons, and funds.

Salan, however, has little choice but to strike within a fortnight—to strike in the sense of the second, or openly "insurrectional," phase. Before the end of that period there will almost surely be a formal peace agreement between Paris and the Algerian Moslem rebels.

When his decisive moment comes it is virtually certain he will begin by launching mass assaults in Algeria by what *Revolutionary Warfare* calls "territorial" and "intervention" units. These will attack the Moslem population in the hopes of embroiling the regular French army by deception and starting an atavistic racial quarrel.

Theoretically it is possible to apply deliberate revolutionary methods for the purposes of counterrevolution; but philosophically this is difficult. For revolution implies adherence to the future while counterrevolution implies adherence to the past.

The periods of history are rare when the past triumphs over the future—and ours is not such an era. So long as de Gaulle can control the essential loyalty of his army, he has won, because his country is with him. So is history. He is confident.

March 1962

Democracies, as we know from ancient Athens, are ungrateful institutions, and the more vibrant their leaders, the more sharply they are attacked. We have only to remember the vivid criticisms of George Washington during his second term or the alacrity with which the English people dismissed Churchill after Germany's defeat.

This tendency, with acid Gallic overtones, is evident in France as de Gaulle seeks finally to impose an end to the Algerian war and internal disaffection. De Gaulle is widely assailed not only by the insurrectionist Secret Army Organization but by political elements of Right, Left, and Center. Yet, curiously, few of these opponents have any positive alternative to offer. And the masses of French people are behind him.

Army leaders complain de Gaulle was brought to power to apply a policy of "French Algeria," which meant incorporating it into France. But de Gaulle, despite one phrase that slipped out in an early speech, has never had this intention. His only thought, when reassuming leadership, was to obtain the most sensible solution possible. Those who read into his statements anything else deliberately deceived themselves.

As long ago as 1944 de Gaulle saw that colonialism was finished and had begun to talk of some kind of commonwealth of independent nations. By 1956, when the nationalist uprising in Algeria was eighteen months old, he saw it would be difficult to arrange a swift peace. He predicted a long and bloody stalemate.

Even then, before he regained the helm, he discerned the basic factors in Algeria: the Algerian people's desire for independence; the injustices they had suffered from past French administrations; the fact that a large number of Frenchmen lived there and the country simply could not survive without them.

After creating his Fifth Republic and studying the conflicting elements, de Gaulle concluded there must be a settlement based on free self-determination. He saw as possible choices: complete "secession" of Algeria from French ties; Frenchification, meaning incorporation as a province, like Normandy; or "association" between a free Algeria and France. What he clearly hopes will eventually result is something between alternatives one and three.

From the start he believed the logic of history and economics would insist on maintaining some form of "association" and basic rights for Europeans in a new Algeria because that new Algeria would need their skills and energies and the aid and capital of France itself.

Within this broad framework de Gaulle worked steadily toward peace. There were only relatively lesser conditions, such as France's keeping economic access to the Sahara and access to Mers-el-Kebir and other militarily important points.

He has, one might say, even less regard for the governing potential of Algerian nationalist politicians than for those of France itself. But he hopes they will begin early to recognize their responsibilities and see the need for sensible relations both with France and with the embittered French Algerians. But he does not intend to be dissuaded from his aims by the rebellious O.A.S.

He is criticized by the French Left for having moved too slowly in making a peace, which such representatives of the

French Left as Pierre Mendès-France and Guy Mollet had been unable to even approach. And he is criticized by the French Right for making peace at all.

Algeria's special illness derives from the fact that in addition to decolonialization's usual agony France's army, despite no lack of bravery or vigor, has not won a war in twenty-three years of steady combat. Cruel awareness of this impels many officers into the disgruntled O.A.S., which, for lack of previous victory against foreign enemies, seems in a sense to desire victory over France itself.

The position of the French Government, trying to achieve the double aim of imposing Algerian peace while limiting internecine bloodshed, becomes increasingly difficult. Sometimes it appears almost paralyzed, as if it practiced a kind of Couéism, not determined action.

One reads of new security attachments brought to Paris; yet homes and offices of those who oppose the O.A.S. continue to be blown up by agents recruited among youngsters, from army deserters, and even from the infamous Katanga corps of *affreux* mercenaries.

Algeria's main cities make bedlam look like placid paradise, and France's administrative corps there seems infected. Last month, when I talked with de Gaulle's Delegate General, Jean Morin, at his fortified headquarters thirty miles from Algiers, my taxi driver was in a special hurry to leave. Morin's own guards had warned him the O.A.S. intended to gun down cars that evening on that very road.

At a reception of senior commanders and civilians, one government official cornered me to extol the O.A.S. The Secret Army seeks to bully public opinion and has already driven out all Italian newspapermen while threatening other members of the brave news corps.

Inside Algeria, as well as inside France, de Gaulle has so far left the job of maintaining security primarily in the hands of various police detachments, preferring, whenever possible, to keep his soldiery from being embroiled in fratricide.

Not only would he prefer to prevent French army units from being forced to fire upon Frenchmen, some of them deserters garbed in stolen military uniforms; he would also like to preserve a strategic reserve for use at the critical moment, when a cease-fire with the Moslem rebels is announced. It is hard, of course, to order brother against brother, no matter how desperate the case. Goethe discerned the essence of wisdom when he said of genius, it is "knowing where to stop." This is the approach hitherto applied by Paris in seeking to avoid bloodshed by restraint. But is not genius, as applied to tragedy of this scale, in knowing when to start, to move against the evil tide?

One should not be deceived by Algeria's sullen calm.

The supreme irony is that an underground guerrilla war has ended only to be replaced by an underground civil war. Until this week the enemies were French and Moslem nationalist soldiers. Perforce the two are becoming co-belligerents in an effort to impose peace on still other Frenchmen.

One can feel sympathy for the European colonists who, having dwelt for years in a kind of isolation ward, dream of reversing history's trend. These are for the most part decent people who have happily deceived themselves with distorted slogans.

They somehow imagine General de Gaulle as a pro-Communist dictator running a France whose public opinion supports their cause. This kind of psychological delusion is not unusual among individuals subjected to great pressures; but it is rare as applied to masses.

That background permitted General Salan's Secret Army more easily to impose its program of "revolutionary warfare," derived from Communist textbooks, although the O.A.S. advertises itself as determined to prevent both Algeria and France from being Communized.

O.A.S. officers acquired the idea of military disobedience from General de Gaulle, who never accepted France's occupation. This, too, is ironic. But neither from the French experience nor the Indochina experience, where they began to dabble in politics, did they learn that "intoxication" is not enough; a revolution must gain popular support. However, the Frenchmen of France and the Moslems of Algeria are for the most part against them.

Another irony is the fact that the only external O.A.S. support comes from Franco's Right-wing opposition. The conspiracy's wet nurse was Franco's brother-in-law and former Foreign Minister (whom he detests), Serrano Suner. Salan, who claims to be a democrat, met his febrile civilian co-plotters initially in Madrid. If an organization leans to the right of Franco it is hard to avoid the label "fascist."

The situation is compounded of further ironies. The O.A.S. pretends it is antiracist and it specializes in murdering Moslems. It learned many of its insidious techniques in Indochina. Yet a principal security detachment used against the O.A.S., the Yatagan Commando, is composed of Vietnamese and French veterans of that unhappy war.

Salan as commander of all French forces in Algeria was unable to defeat the Moslem rebels. Nevertheless he now aspires to defeat both them and France. His very first pronouncement, eleven months ago, talked of saving "France and Christianity." But this conspiratorial veteran, erstwhile opium smoker and consultant of astrologers, chooses Communist methods for his Christian crusade.

The cruellest irony is the shattering of de Gaulle's belief that the army in France is apolitical and is "always for order and *la Patrie*."

We ponder ironies and we wait. The moment draws near for Salan to make his move in the bitter land called "Barbary" by the Romans. If he does make his move, that is. One is minded of Cavafy, the great Greek poet, who wrote:

"Because night is here but the barbarians have not come./Some people arrived from the frontiers,/and they said that there are no longer any barbarians./And now what shall become of us without any barbarians?/Those people were a kind of solution."

In terms of the tragic civil war now being fought between Frenchmen on Algeria's bloody ground, March 23, 1962, may be considered in one sense comparable to that sad date in United States history, April 12, 1861, when South Carolina batteries fired on Fort Sumter.

For March 23, members of General Salan's insurrectional Secret Army opened fire on regular troops, killing several. This started Frenchman fighting Frenchman, as, a century earlier, Sumter similarly touched off fratricide. Of course, the French family conflict is confined to Algeria only and one prays it will be of short duration and on a small scale.

Friday's brief, fatal skirmish was a major O.A.S. mistake. The O.A.S. had hoped by its "intoxication" propaganda and by stimulating racial fracases between Europeans and Moslems to win the allegiance of some regular French units. When they themselves slaughtered soldiers of France they seemingly shattered any chance that such tactics might succeed.

The loyalty of certain elite units and certain professional officers had been in doubt during recent years.

The Foreign Legion posed a specially delicate problem because, under French law, it cannot be stationed in metropolitan France. Its excellent fighting men, including a disproportionate number of Germans, had sometimes shown more loyalty to their commanders and their own *esprit de corps* than to the state. Therefore de Gaulle, following the April 1961 *Putsch,* gradually shifted Legion units to the extreme eastern and western frontiers of Algeria, far away from the trouble centers of Algiers and Oran where the O.A.S. is strongest.

As armistice negotiations in Evian approached their climax earlier this month, de Gaulle apparently played a clever trick designed to frustrate any thought of trouble from the Legionnaires. At least this would appear to be the logical interpretation of two curious events.

First of all, the Moslem F.L.N., just before the cease-fire, began an artillery bombardment of French positions from bases along the Tunisian border. Legion troops, among others, were moved yet farther eastward to riposte.

Almost simultaneously reports were spread of heavy F.L.N. concentrations in Morocco allegedly preparing to penetrate Algeria from the west. Legion units were sent from their traditional base at Sidi-Bel-Abbès to block this rumored threat. In each case, on the east and on the west, fuel for Legion transport was strictly rationed so that any conceivably doubtful unit would find it difficult to make its way to the Algiers-Oran area.

So now the O.A.S. finds itself far more isolated than its proponents of "revolutionary warfare" had hoped. The Pretorian formations are physically beyond temptation. And angry French soldiers and gendarmes have cut off one O.A.S. stronghold in Algiers and invaded another in Oran, seizing a main conspirator, General Jouhaud.

Meanwhile, French stock has soared in the Arab world. De Gaulle has proved he meant what he said about peace and self-determination for Algeria. Throughout Islam, where the F.L.N. had won much support in its war against France, de Gaulle is now seen as a just man true to his word. Thus overnight, despite lingering Arab resentment at the special Franco-Israeli friendship, Paris has regained Arab respect.

April 1962

In terms of party politics President de Gaulle's decision to name Georges Pompidou Prime Minister does not make sense. M. Pompidou has no electoral backing, is not a politician, and is little known. He is also a director of the Rothschild Bank. In contemporary France the Rothschild political stigma is approximately equivalent to that of the Rockefellers in the U.S.A. fifty years ago.

But de Gaulle is confident his own mystical link with the French people obviates customary dependence on direct party support. He has allowed neither Pompidou's anonymity nor his financial connections to deter him from putting the right man in the right place. And his intuitive assumption that France supports him has been confirmed overwhelmingly in a referendum.

Pompidou served de Gaulle as a personal executive intermittently from France's liberation until the General returned to power in 1958; and in so doing he had constant contact with politicians. He is what is called in France an intellectual and a technician. He is cool, unflustered, and the last man, for example, to be concerned by Left-wing attacks on him as a Rothschild "tool." He has the manner of authority.

He is a large man with soft voice and manner. The only hint of inner nervousness is his habit of chain-smoking cigarettes. He is worldly, competent, and not in the least afraid to shoulder any burden handed him.

Personally closer than his predecessor, Debré, to de Gaulle, he is at home in literary circles (being himself a respected scholar and author), the worlds of high finance, diplomacy, and action. De Gaulle entirely trusts him. He used Pompidou to handle particularly confidential aspects of his Algerian negotiations.

One might describe Pompidou as more liberal than Debré. He has never doubted the need for civilian government to establish firm control over an unruly army. He saw the necessity for an Algerian accommodation long before his predecessor. He does not, unlike certain excitable Frenchmen, think the Moslem nationalists have been "captured" by Communism.

He is confident that traditional economic links between France and an independent Algeria will restore close friendship despite years of bloodshed and will insure a place for the bewildered French minority. He has seen burgeoning Africa waver toward the East but believes it will swing Westward.

Pompidou has remarked in the past that there are no problems of substance between Paris and Washington that cannot, in the long run, be solved. He is delighted that, despite Franco-American disputes, de Gaulle seems to remain extraordinarily popular with Americans.

He was once worried by diabolical rumors that American agents were supporting de Gaulle's opponents in the hopes of replacing him because of his NATO attitude. But Pompidou, a realist, looked into these tales and concluded they were false as well as foolish.

Before visiting the U.S.A. in 1960, Pompidou saw both de Gaulle and his Foreign Minister to assure himself that French policy was still founded on NATO attachments despite differences in approach. He wanted to be able to answer questions honestly and accurately. He was reassured.

One could call Pompidou neither pro-American nor anti-American; he is a Frenchman, a European, a Westerner. He understands why Washington may dislike de Gaulle's insistence on French national nuclear power because he has admitted France might similarly not like to see an independent Italian atomic force.

Nevertheless, he believes with de Gaulle that Europe must have a nuclear capacity controlled by Europeans. Without this, he has said, were Moscow to exert immense pressure in this area, future Americans might repeat slogans similar to that once heard in Britain: "Is it worth dying for Danzig?" Would the United States retaliate against anything short of a direct attack against North America?

Pompidou is a modern man. He realizes de Gaulle's great popular appeal has been helped by the use of television. He hopes to improve the status of workers by giving them a larger share of profits in private enterprise rather than by toying with forms of socialism.

His imminent appointment marks a change in emphasis

by de Gaulle. Henceforth the stress will be less on Algeria and more on constitutional reform, Europe's future, Western development, and France's economic expansion. This is Stage Two of the Fifth Republic.

De Gaulle has won his war against the O.A.S. but not the final battle. There is going to be underground opposition to the Fifth Republic both here and in Algeria for some time to come.

In France revolutionary steps inevitably provoke counter-revolution. And the release of Algeria to independence is a revolutionary step. This mere fact was bound to touch off reaction, just as, in the past, there have been similar reactions from the Right-wing *Ligue,* the *Fronde,* by the *ultras* of the Restoration, General Boulanger's plot, and the *Cagoulards* of the nineteen-thirties.

The O.A.S. doesn't realize it but what de Gaulle calls *"l'Algérie de papa"* is gone. There will, tragically, be more violence before this is hammered into General Salan's nostalgic mind. There will be massive sabotage. For months tons of dynamite have been secreted near the oil refinery of Hassi Messaoud in the Sahara.

The O.A.S. hopes to try to stage a Götterdämmerung in France itself. Salan orders that leading Frenchmen be murdered, innocents attacked, grenades tossed into cinemas, as was done in Indochina by the Vietminh Communists.

Salan would like to bring what he calls his war to France itself. And some politicians who at least sympathize with his objectives, such as the absent Soustelle and Bidault (the former Premier who has fled abroad), appear to rally to this dead-end goal.

But they allow emotion to confuse logic. The French support de Gaulle's, not Salan's, Algerian policy. O.A.S. agents are being remorselessly hunted down and have suffered shattering blows. Nevertheless, Salan pipe dreams that he may achieve his goals in France itself. But this is as insane as it is hideous. A resolute French Government and the huge majority of French people oppose his aims and are ready to resist.

O.A.S. agents include gutter fascists, ordinary gunmen, and deluded idealists. They may try to slay French leaders or French civilians in France as they have slain them in Algeria. These are battles yet to come. But they cannot win the war.

The O.A.S. calls its murder gangs "commandos" and dresses its schemes in such highfaluting language as "revolutionary warfare" and "parallel hierarchies." But it never learned lesson one from Mao—"revolutionary warfare" requires both a base and forward thinking, not backward looking.

The only bases left to the Secret Army are the beleaguered cities of Algiers and Oran. Little by little, despite their ruthless violence, its terrorists are being winkled out of Algiers. Oran is different, for Oran has long been isolated from reality.

Oran contains more Europeans than Moslems, a polyglot mélange. It has a penchant for dream life. There will be a grim and sanguinary battle in Oran before the insurrection ends.

But de Gaulle has already squeezed that insurrection down to coastline cities. When the O.A.S. tried a campaign in the countryside it was squashed. Algiers and Oran are no proper base.

The Secret Army has lost the initiative, one essential "revolutionary warfare" factor. It is losing morale, a second. It never had mass sympathy in France, and sympathy among Algerian Europeans is slowly starting to flake off.

O.A.S. operational doctrine would seem founded on misapplication of the Vietminh manual on guerrilla war. This advises: "Mislead the enemy, make him negligent, and then attack unexpectedly." But Salan operates in reverse. He has misled his own forces and they have been negligent. All they can still apply is the tactic of unexpected attack or murder.

"Attack, destroy, and withdraw," counsels Mao's manual. But the O.A.S. has no place to withdraw beyond Algiers and Oran. It is trying to withdraw to France itself by grouping its agents and sympathizers for a last-ditch bitter stand. But even if its gunmen produce tragedy again, their cause is ended before they begin to shoot. For this savage conspiracy seeks with a handful of men to halt history. History has already passed them by.

May 1962

But French history sometimes reverses rather than repeats itself. One has only to compare contemporary headlines with those of four years ago to confirm this postulate. The names are the same; the positions are astonishingly different.

In May, 1958, General de Gaulle had just returned to Paris from self-imposed country exile and announced he was ready to resume power. General Salan, heading an Algiers military conspiracy, boasted: "I have provisionally taken into my hands the destinies of French Algeria." He acclaimed de Gaulle.

Algeria, de Gaulle, and Salan remain big news. So do the French army and its conspiratorial tastes. But the context has wholly changed. De Gaulle is not ready to resume power; he holds it. And he believes this demands more, not less, government in France.

In one of his rare press conferences he has repeated his singularly personal views of policy and aspirations. Quite as strongly as when he returned to Paris four years ago he has shown his determination to recapture for France a position of ascendancy. But now he is in a position to apply his thoughts. And what Washington once deemed preposterous it now deems arrogant or absurd.

De Gaulle is resolved to reassert the skills and energies of Europe—a Europe he views as extending from the Urals to the Atlantic—under French leadership, a leadership he intends to press despite strong opposition. He wants Paris to speak in Western councils with a Continental voice.

De Gaulle is withdrawing his troops from festering Algeria and turning them into his old dream, a professional army (about which he once wrote a book). He hopes this professional army will be not only competent to protect France but also content to serve it, not to try to master it.

General Ailleret, father of France's atom bomb and recent commander of French forces in Algeria, will become Chief of Staff. De Gaulle hopes, with these atomic toys, to rid the army of those psychotic complexes symbolized by Salan on trial in the Court of Justice.

The French Left accepted de Gaulle's return in the first place as an alternative to military rule. The French Right accepted de Gaulle's return as an alternative to chaos and a popular front. Both extremes consider themselves deceived but the vast if indeterminate French Center is behind him.

Salan, that other headline figure four years ago, was in the prisoner's dock as de Gaulle spoke in the Presidential Palace.

Salan, who hailed and sought to dominate de Gaulle, has become a symbol of the defeated past. Salan represents the counterrevolutionary Secret Army that has already shrugged him off as a tarnished vestige. Meanwhile, the O.A.S. moves from action to reaction. Having virtually lost its battle to keep outmoded privileges in Algeria, it seeks to overthrow progress in France itself.

Salan's former tools, colonels and frustrated politicians, carry on his cause, intensifying their fury while ignoring their discarded chief. They no longer want just a French Algeria. They want an Algerian France.

They have neither held Algeria nor won France. Yet they threaten the possibility and hope that, a year or two hence, the two nations can revive friendship and work together as partners.

For O.A.S. terrorism may well insure that the vindictive French Algerians will be expelled to their motherland. This would weaken the new North African state. And it would produce an embittered political minority in France to join the entrenched Right in opposing progress long after both de Gaulle and Salan are gone.

Unless present trends are soon checked one may be able to predict future reversals just as it was possible four years ago to discern essentials of today's strange tragedy.

Index

Adenauer, Konrad, 6, 159, 186
Ailleret, Charles, 25, 221
Algeria: colonists of, 23, 91, 104, 106-08, 174, 211-12; French civil war in, 213-14, 215; guerrilla operations in, 22, 27, 104; independence movement in (1947), 14; as major active battle front, 104, 144; Moslem population of, 104, 174; and NATO, 173; number of French troops in (1957), 26; partition of, 175; possible confederation with Tunisia and Morocco, 172; insurrection in (1958), 53, 55, 56-58, 59, 147, 185, (1961), 166-69, 179, 214; Revolutionary Committees of Public Safety in, 93
Algeria National Movement, 27, 29
Algerian Army of National Liberation (A.L.N.), 111, 112
Algerian Committee of Public Safety, 58
Algerian Communist party, 28
Algerian Home Guard, 138
Algiers, 53, 57, 62, 63, 124, 142, 148, 150, 191; Radio, 76; violence in, 201-03, 205, 219
Alleg, Henri, 44
Arab League, 14, 175

Army, French: "activists" in, 132; Communist operational methods used by, 124, 132, 133, 138; defeats of, during two decades, 102, 124, 210; de Gaulle's views of, 75, 89, 99, 100-01; entry into politics, 60, 90-91, 105, 212, 213; General Staff of, 25, 26, 121; governmental control over, reasserted by de Gaulle, 93, 148; paratroopers of, 132; and plots against de Gaulle, 122, 123, 124, 136, 142, 149, 166-67, 205-07; insurrection in Algeria (1958), 53, 55, 56-58, 59, 147, 185, (1961), 166-69, 179, 214
Arrighi, Pascal, 63
As France Goes, 50
Atomic-energy program, French, 26, 30, 36, 87-88, 95, 140, 161, 221
Auriol, Vincent, 15
Azzedine, Major, 112

Bailly, Paul, 131
Ben Bella, Mohammed, 198
Ben Khedda, Benyoussef, 188, 197
Berber Kabyles, 108, 112
Bergson, Henri, 151, 194

Berlin crisis, 139
Bidault, Georges, 56, 122, 137, 218
Bigeard, Marcel, 132
Bizerte, Tunisia, 77, 95
Bled, 106, 108, 110
Bonn, West Germany, 21, 30, 68
Boulanger, General G.E.J.M., 14, 218
Bourgès-Maunoury, Maurice, 50, 156
Bourguiba, Habib, 22, 32, 36, 78, 157, 158, 172
Brussels Pact, 17
Buffet, Bernard, 49

Cagoulards, 136, 218
Cairo, Egypt, 14, 15, 157, 171
Camus, Albert, 205
Canard Enchaîné, Le, 134
Castro, Fidel, 186
Catholicism, French, 51
Center, French, 50, 51, 53
Central Intelligence Agency, U.S., 67, 167, 168, 169
Chaban-Delmas, Jacques, 49, 60
Challe, Maurice, xi, 61, 121, 168, 206
Chassin, Lionel, 53, 132
Chevigné, Pierre de, 60, 61
China, 171
Churchill, Winston, 5, 8, 18, 23, 69
Colombey-les-Deux-Eglises, 6, 7, 18
Common Market, European, 116, 160, 200
Communist party, French: and de Gaulle, 79, 80, 86, 89-90, 166; tactics of, 83-85, 125; voting strength of, 37, 50-51, 79, 85

Condorcet, Marquis de, 81
Congo, 160, 181
Constitution, new French, 88-89
Corsica, 63, 76, 100
Coty, René, 45, 54, 64
Cuba, 169
Cyprus, 31, 104, 105, 106, 169, 175

Dahlab, Saad, 188, 197
Debré, Michel, x, xii, 5, 216
De Gaulle, Charles: and army, views of, 75, 89, 99, 100-01; background of, 17; as Centrist, 3, 80, 81, 221; character of, 5, 8, 18, 21, 68-69, 165, 193; and Communism, 79, 80, 86, 89-90, 166; autocratic intentions denied by, 70; on "drama" in history, 46, 53, 64; and Eisenhower, 66, 115, 117-18, 119-20, 142, 143, 159, 161; Free French movement organized by, 41, 45, 75; on French grandeur, 70, 95, 101, 114, 141; fundamental policy of, on European security, 21; insurrection in army quelled by (1961), 166-69, 179, 214; and Kennedy, 159-61, 167, 168, 185, 186, 187; and Khrushchev, 139, 140, 141; and labor-capital *associations,* 7, 24; leadership qualities of, 165; as literary stylist, 69; literary tastes of, 194; memoirs of, 6, 23; musical tastes of, 194; National Liberation Front approached by, 93-94, 121; nationalism of, 87, 88; NATO, views of, 94-95, 114-16; and new Constitution, 88-89, 135;

nuclear program favored by, 26, 87-88, 140, 161, 221; plots against, by army, 122, 123, 124, 136, 142, 149, 166-67, 205-07; Pompidou appointed by, 215-17; popularity of, 92, 150, 191, 208; as President, 63-65, 101, 113-14, 125-28; program for Algeria, 77, 79, 89, 208-09; program for French leadership in Europe, 221; program for internal reforms, 79, 82, 217, 218; and insurrection in Algeria (1958), 53, 55, 56-58, 59, 147, 185; referendum on Algerian policy of, 92, 153-54, 156; regroupment policy of, 192; respect for, in Arab world, 215; on role of crises in national affairs, 70; and Roosevelt, 18, 114, 117; Secret Army Organization's attacks on, 208; on trip to Algeria, 152; and United Nations, 94, 95, 160; United States' attitude toward, 66-67, 116, 117, 118, 119, 121, 136, 142, 143, 161, 167, 185, 186, 187

Dienbienphu, 82
Ducasse, Louis, 93, 132
Duclos, Jacques, 86
Dulles, John Foster, 49, 66
Duval, Léon-Etienne, 205

East Germany, 21
Eastland, James O., 155
Edge of the Sword, 126
Egypt, 26, 34, 158, 197
Eighteenth Brumaire, 55
Eisenhower, Dwight D., and de Gaulle, 66, 115, 117-18, 119-20, 142, 143, 159, 161
Eliot, T. S., 139
Ely, Paul, 53, 57, 60, 61, 76, 91, 121, 131
European Common Market, 116, 160, 200
European Defense Community, 66
Evian-les-Bains, 170, 172, 174, 175, 214

Faguet, Emile, 165
Fascism, French, 80, 125, 212
Faure, Jacques, 137
Faure, Maurice, 49
Fifth Republic, 89, 102, 113, 118, 123, 125, 135, 145-47, 181, 184, 205, 209, 218
First Republic, 55, 135
Foreign Legion, 179, 214
Fourth Republic, 7, 18, 23, 29, 35, 46, 50, 51, 52; destruction of, desired by Moscow, 68; in Indochina war, 90, 102; overthrow of, 61-65, 76, 82, 86, 87, 100
France Against Herself, 50
France 1940-1955, 50
Franco, Francisco, 56, 212
Free French movement, 41, 45, 75

Gaillard, Félix, 47, 49, 50, 60, 61, 62
Gajewski, Stanislaw, 67, 68
Gardes, Jean, 180
Gavin, James M., 167
Gilles, Jean, 53, 93
Giraud, Henri, 75
Girondism, 55
Godard, Yves, 167, 180

Goldwater, Barry M., 155
Great Britain: colonial disentanglement of, 31; and NATO, 95, 96
Greece, partisan movement in, 28, 170
Gribius, André, 137
Guerrilla warfare, 22, 27, 29, 104
Guerrilla Warfare According to the Communist School, 181

Hadj, Messali, 78
Hitler, Adolf, 155

India, 30, 31, 35, 42, 105, 176
Indochina, 23, 31, 42, 60, 90, 102, 103, 132, 181, 206, 212, 218
Iraq, 34, 157
Islam, 14, 15, 78
Israel, 215
Izvestia, 169

Jacobinism, 55
Jebb, Gladwyn, 67
Joan of Arc, 14
Jordan, 34, 157
Jouhaud, Edmond, x, xi, xii, 93, 180, 204, 205
Juin, Alphonse-Pierre, 44, 59, 120, 179

Kennedy, John F., and de Gaulle, 159-61, 167, 168, 185, 186, 187
Khrushchev, Nikita, 88, 185, 186; and de Gaulle, 139, 140, 141
Krim, Belkacem, 197

Lacheroy, Charles, 206
Lagaillarde, Pierre, 132, 137, 149

Lamartine, Alphonse de, 81
Laos, 169
Lawrence, T. E., 27-28
Lebanon, 42, 157
Left, French, 50, 51, 52, 80, 84, 221
Lenin, Nikolai, 90, 140
Le Pen, Jean-Marie, 132
Lesson in Revolutionary Warfare, A, 206, 207
Levant, 23
L'Express, 44
Libya, 14, 157
Lorraine, Cross of, 5, 23
Luethy, Herbert, 50

Macmillan, Harold, 159, 161, 186
Madagascar, 152
Maghreb, 35, 158
Malaya, 31, 170
Malraux, André, 9, 81, 82, 83, 84
Manchester *Guardian*, 48
Mao Tse-tung, 28, 90, 124, 138, 181, 182, 219, 220
Marshall Plan, 17
Martin, André, 61
Massu, Jacques, ix, 53, 56, 61, 62, 76, 102-03, 112, 122, 132, 136, 142
Melouza massacre, 27
Mendès-France, Pierre, 210
Menemençioglu, Numan, 67
Mers-el-Kebir, 170, 175, 189, 209
Méry-Beuve, Hubert, 55
Mirambeau, Henri, 137
Moch, Jules, 62
Mollet, Guy, 210
Monde, Le, 168
Morin, Jean, 210
Morocco, 14, 23, 29, 32, 34, 35, 42, 43, 56, 106; F.L.N.'s de-

pendence on bases in, 103, 104, 105, 170; history of independent self-rule in, 78; possible confederation with Algeria and Tunisia, 172

Naguib, Mohammed, 133, 197, 198
Napoleon I, 42, 46, 55, 87, 100
Napoleon III, 42, 43
Nasser, Gamel Abdel, 44, 111, 133, 157, 158, 172, 197, 198
National Liberation Front (F.L.N.), 29, 134, 144, 188, 189, 190, 191, 192, 193, 214; Communist penetration of, 28-29, 148, 197-98; de Gaulle's offer to negotiate with, 93-94, 121; dependence on bases in Tunisia and Morocco, 103, 104, 105, 170; terrorist tactics of, 27, 99, 150
Nehru, Jawaharlal, 36
Neuwirth, Lucien, 58
Norstad, Lauris, 173
North Atlantic Treaty Organization (NATO), 22, 26, 30, 35, 49, 66, 68, 80, 86, 105, 138, 217; and Algeria, 173; atomic striking power of, 115-16; de Gaulle's views of, 94-95, 114-16; and United States, 95, 96, 114, 115, 116, 119; and Soviet Union, 148

Oder-Neisse Line, 117, 141
Oran, 150, 151, 175, 185, 190, 191, 204, 219

Palestine, 14, 31, 105, 176, 205
Paris, demonstrations in, 45-46, 47, 48, 59

Pavlov, Ivan, 206
Pétain, Henri Philippe, 6, 42, 76, 100, 102
Petit, André, 57
Pflimlin, Pierre, ix, 60, 61, 62
Pinay, Antoine, 153, 154
Pompidou, Georges, xii, 215-17
Pondicherry, 35, 152
Popular Front, 51
Poujade, Pierre, 25, 124, 153

Quai d'Orsay, 20, 22, 190
Quaroni, Pietro, 67
Question, La, 44

Rabah, Zerrari, 112
Radio Algiers, 76
Rally of the French People (R.P.F.), 16, 19, 21, 80
Rape of the Masses, The, 206
Republican Committee of Defense, 85
Right, French, 50, 51, 53, 63, 80, 93, 136, 154-56, 166, 172, 221, 222; and army, 59, 122; and de Gaulle, 155; de Gaulle's view of, 76; size of, 155
Robespierre, Maximilien François, 87
Roosevelt, Franklin D., and de Gaulle, 18, 114, 117
Russia: Algerian insurrectionists supported by, 148, 171; destruction of Fourth Republic desired by, 68; East German state created by, 21; and NATO, 148

Sagan, Françoise, 49

Sahara, 168, 199, 200, 209, 218; atomic explosion in, 116; oil found in, 188, 198, 199
St. Cyr, 132
St. Laurent, Yves, 49
Sakiet Sidi Youssef, French bombing of, ix, 31-34, 42, 65
Salan, Raoul, ix, x, xi, xii, 56, 58, 60, 61, 91, 149, 153, 180, 185, 203, 204, 205, 206, 207, 212, 213, 218, 219, 220, 221-22
Sartre, Jean-Paul, 44, 56
Saudi Arabia, 157
Savary, Alain, 134
Schoenbrun, David, 50
SEATO, 49
Secret Army Organization (O.A.S.), 179, 180, 183, 184, 187, 190, 191, 192, 193, 208, 210; Communist operational methods used by, 181-82, 206, 207, 212, 213, 219, 220; membership of, 203; violence by, 3, 8, 201-03, 204, 218, 219, 222
SHAPE, 115, 116, 186
Slimane, Major, 173
Soustelle, Jacques, 53, 57, 78, 137, 153, 156, 218
South Vietnam, 35
Spain, 149, 153, 212
Speidel, Hans, 117
Stalin, Josef, 69, 140
Suez, 25, 60, 158
Suner, Serrano, 149, 212
Susini, Jean-Jacques, 203, 204
Syria, 34, 42

Tchakotine, Serge, 206
Third Republic, 19, 35, 50, 102, 135, 155

Thomazo, Jean, 53, 76, 93, 100, 132
Thompson, James Matthew, 55
Thorez, Maurice, 83, 84, 85, 86
Trinquier, Roger, 93, 132
Tunisia, 14, 22, 29, 42, 43, 106, 125, 148; F.L.N.'s dependence on bases in, 103, 104, 105, 170; French bombing of, 31-34, 42, 65; history of independent self-rule in, 78; possible confederation with Algeria and Morocco, 172
Tyler, William, 186-87

United Arab Republic, 158
United Nations, 94, 95, 160
United States: attitude toward de Gaulle, 66-67, 116, 117, 118, 119, 121, 136, 142, 143, 161, 167, 185, 186, 187, 221; and French Center, 51; and NATO, 95, 96, 114, 115, 116, 119; policy toward North Africa, 22, 119, 120, 121, 168-69; resentment against, by A.L.N., 112-13; and United Nations, 160

Vichy France, 6, 51
Vietminh, 44, 181, 218
Vinogradov, Sergei, 67, 68

Werth, Alexander, 50
West Germany, 20, 30, 96, 116, 117
Wilson, Woodrow, 32

Yatagan Commando, 212
Yugoslavia, 27, 28, 29, 34

Zeller, André, x, xi, 93, 205